SINCLAIR COLLECTIBLES

Wayne Henderson
&
Scott Benjamin

Schiffer Publishing Ltd
77 Lower Valley Road, Atglen, PA 19310

Library of Congress Catalog Card Number: 96-72026.

Printed in China
ISBN: 0-7643-0193-4

Book Design by Audrey L. Whiteside

Published by Schiffer Publishing, Ltd.
77 Lower Valley Road

Atglen, PA 19310
Phone: (610) 593-1777
Fax: (610) 593-2002
E-mail: schifferbk@aol.com
Please write for a free catalog.
This book may be purchased from the publisher.
Please include $2.95 for shipping.
Try your bookstore first.

We are interested in hearing from authors
with book ideas on related subjects.

Contents

Introduction 4
Chapter One: 1916-1920 Formation of an Industry Giant 5
Chapter Two: 1920-1932 Innovative Marketing & "H-C" 13
- Sinclair Foreign Marketing 35
Chapter Three: 1932-1946 Growth Through Acquisition 37
- Richfield Oil Company of New York 80
Chapter Four: 1946-1959 Refinement of an Image 85
- Experimental Images 123
Chapter Five: 1959-1970 Dino Era & Lean Years 127
Chapter Six: 1970-1976 Atlantic Richfield and Sinclair 149
Chapter Seven: 1976-1996 Rebuilding an Independent Giant 153
Appendix One: Sinclair & Richfield Pump Color Schemes 157
Appendix Two: Quick Reference Guide 158
Index 160

Introduction

The authors wish to thank all their many contributors to this publication. First and foremost, our thanks goes to Jackie Knott of Carrollton, Missouri, for allowing us to photograph his extensive collection of Sinclair memorabilia, including his many rare and unique items. Special acknowledgment also goes to Messaros Photography and Vasco Martin for their photography work in this book. We also wish to thank the many subscribers to *Petroleum Collectibles Monthly* for their support and their continued contributions to this and other projects. Should anyone reading this work have further information or items not pictured in this book, particularly unusual Sinclair globes or signage, please contact the authors so that your item may be included in any future updates of this work. Contact Scott Benjamin of Oil Company Collectibles at the address shown in the quick reference guide at the end of this book.

CHAPTER ONE 1916-1920

Formation of an Industry Giant

The largest and most powerful creatures to ever roam the earth were the dinosaurs. They are generally considered to be fierce, fast moving, and dominant over all other creatures they came in contact with. It is also believed that they demonstrated many of these traits from the moment they were hatched.

Many millenniums later a hard driving young man, working in a chaotic industry, founded a company that also demonstrated many of these same tendencies. From its incorporation it was large in scope, fierce in competition with others, moved from conception to a national existence within a few months, and dominated many of the aspects of the industry that it operated within. Several years after its founding, the corporation chose the dinosaur for its trademark. Though chosen at the time primarily to symbolize the age of the crude oil used in its lubricants, those of us that have the advantage of historical perspective can see the many other aspects of the company that the dinosaur represents so well.

This photo shows an early Sinclair station, 1916-1920, presumably in New York. *Jackie Knott Collection.*

I am speaking, of course, of Sinclair. Sinclair was a late-comer to the U.S. petroleum industry, having been assembled in 1916 from various individual holdings controlled by Harry F. Sinclair. Mr. Sinclair was born on the Kansas frontier in 1876, and frontier life throughout his young years taught him many of the lessons that eventually proved necessary for success. Young Harry was slated to enter into the family business, a pharmacy, but as fate would have it, the pharmacy was lost in a speculation during an economic downturn in 1896. At age twenty, casting around for something to do, Harry noticed the growing opportunity in oil exploration.

Oil exploration, particularly in the mid-continent area, was not for the fainthearted. Fortunes could be made and lost in a single day, as crude prices fluctuated wildly. To make a profit one needed a lot of luck, access to ready capital, a working knowledge of whom could be trusted, along with all the other basic skills necessary to be a leader to those around you. Speculators thrived only when as leaders, not followers. Harry Sinclair possessed all of these traits, along with a willingness to work hard and perseverance when negotiating. He moved quickly, wisely invested money for his partners, and had attracted the attention of oil men far more experienced than he. Even more importantly, he had attracted willing investors, and in his first ten years in oil exploration he had netted his investors huge returns...and found himself amply rewarded. As his own investments in his speculations grew, Harry found himself in a position where each successive move was easier than the one previous, as banks were willing to lend to a man with substantial interest in an investment and a proven track record of successes. Up until this time Harry's companies had been largely one-lease operations. However, a series of successes in 1904 and 1905 provided sufficient capital for his investment in the Glenn Pool, Oklahoma oil fields. With everything that could be found to invest, Harry gambled it all on Oklahoma's first big oil field, a gamble that proved to be a sure bet. Harry Sinclair found himself a millionaire, and in control of interests worth far more.

His speculator's nose eventually led him to the Oklahoma oil-boom town of Tulsa, where he took stock of his interests. Within several years Harry had gone from holding only passing interests in his own operations to having control of exploration crews and equipment, terminals and storage facilities, and even a bank. With even better access to investment capital, he began purchasing bargain crude from the overworked oil fields at Cushing, Oklahoma. Oil was simply stored until marketing conditions were most favorable. In the meantime he had invested, along with mentor and early financial backer J. M.

One of Sinclair's earliest lubricants trademarks was "Shamrock." Shown here are several Sinclair Shamrock grease containers. $350 each. *Jackie Knott Collection.*

Cudahy, in a small refining & marketing operation aptly named Cudahy Refining. Through Cudahy, the investors were able to get immediate return on investment, as stored crude could be refined and marketed through a series of bulk stations to an ever growing number of automobile operators. The Cudahy operation had also excelled in lubricants development and was marketing an oil specifically for use in automotive engines. That engine oil, Opaline, would continue to be marketed for most of the next sixty years.

In an era that has seen conglomerates form with many diverse, and indeed unrelated profit centers, it seems so strange to consider a group of interdependent operations, engaged in various aspects of the same business, owned or controlled by the same small group of people, that existed only as separate entities with NO central structure whatsoever. But, as 1916 began, that is just what existed with the various operations owned, controlled, or managed by Sinclair. It was the largest "non-company" of its kind.

Sinclair inherited the "Opaline" trademark with the purchase of Cudahy Refining Company's marketing operations. This 8" by 15" tin-litho sign advertises Cudahy Opaline and dates from around 1914-1915. $600-$800. *Jackie Knott Collection.*

Recognizing the opportunity to take advantage of an overwhelming supply of cheap crude from mid-continent overproduction, Harry Sinclair moved fast. Individually his holdings, productive as they were, were simply not suitable as collateral, particularly to bankers unaccustomed to the rough-and-tumble ways of the oil fields. Big-city bankers knew only how to read a balance sheet. So, in order to gain that "measure" of respectability, Sinclair consolidated all of his holdings—each individual lease, pipeline, terminal, refinery plant, the Cudahy bulk stations—and combined it all into a new entity, Sinclair Oil and Refining Company. On May 1, 1916, the giant was born.

Close up of the automobile scene on the Cudahy Opaline sign. *Jackie Knott Collection.*

Initially more imagination than fact, since little had changed from the time when each entity operated as a separate profit center, the new corporation was at least enough to impress Wall Street and the big-city bankers. For the first time, expansion capital, in essentially unlimited amounts, was available. Access to crude was the secret. All other facilities—storage, pipelines, rail transportation, or refineries—could be secured, but without the crude it was all useless. Sinclair quickly purchased producing crude oil operations throughout the mid-continent area. Depressed pricing dictated the expansion funds would go far. Then, with his infrastructure in place, Sinclair began the most ambitious expansion that any of the mid-continent companies would ever attempt.

Sinclair one gallon cans. On the left is a Sinclair "Mercury" can from prior to 1920, and on the right is a generic locally-filled can from the 1930s. $25-$100. *Jackie Knott Collection.*

In sight of the enormous Standard Oil Company of Indiana refinery complex at Whiting, Indiana, Sinclair purchased land and began construction of a refinery complex that came to be known as "East Chicago." Far south, construction began on a pipeline from the heart of Sinclair production in Oklahoma, a pipeline designed to transport Oklahoma crude to East Chicago. Chicago and its suburbs were identified as a target market for retail expansion. With the infrastructure in place, Sinclair began market expansion, purchasing gasoline marketing operations throughout the country. The trademark "Sinco" was adopted, and filling stations or curb pumps displaying globes reading "Sinclair Gasoline" were to be found throughout the mid-continent area and as far east as upstate New York.

By 1918 the pipeline was complete, the East Chicago refinery was operable, and a new facility at Kansas City was nearing completion. Key management was in place, much of it having been inherited from Cudahy and other predecessors. The refining expertise of former Cudahy employee W. H. Isom allowed Sinclair to fully develop a refining process using equipment of their own design. Again concentrating on crude oil production and purchase and refinery throughout, in the years before 1920 Sinclair found its niche as a refining and marketing powerhouse. Sinclair "Sinco" gasoline and Opaline Motor Oils (a brand name inherited from Cudahy) were among the most well received products among motorists of the day.

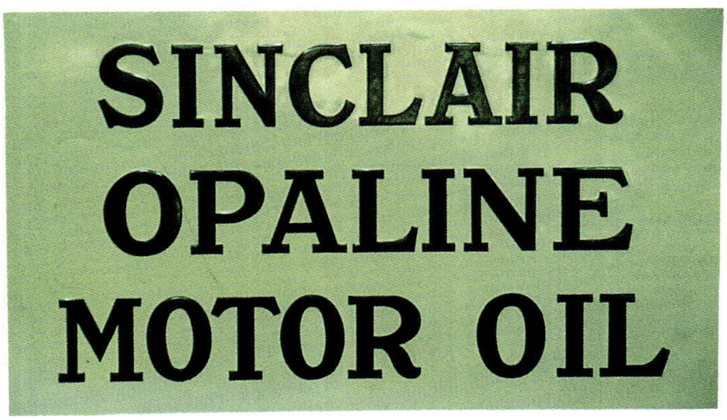

This is one of the earliest examples of Sinclair dealer identification signage. These tin litho signs were used at curb pump stations, country stores, and other locations where Sinclair products were sold that did not merit a standard identification sign. $200-$300. *Jackie Knott Collection.*

Sinclair then further solidified its crude oil position with the development of crude exploration along the Gulf Coast. A separate corporation, Sinclair Gulf Corporation, was established to develop this exploration opportunity. Created in much the same way that the original Sinclair operation had been, in the consolidation of individual bits and pieces, the control of crude oil production proved very beneficial to the growth-minded operation.

East Coast expansion began in this era as well, as Sinclair Gulf operated some Atlantic Coast terminals. In order to take advantage of this ever-growing market, Sinclair purchased Union Petroleum Company, whose operations included what would become Sinclair's Marcus Hook, Pennsylvania, refinery, as well as a line of highest quality lubricants.

Continuing a string of successful exploration ventures, Sinclair entered Mexico, and within several years Mexican crude would prove to be very important in Sinclair's Gulf Coast and Caribbean operations. All Sinclair operations were brought together in 1919 under the banner "Sinclair Consolidated Oil Corporation." An oil giant had been born.

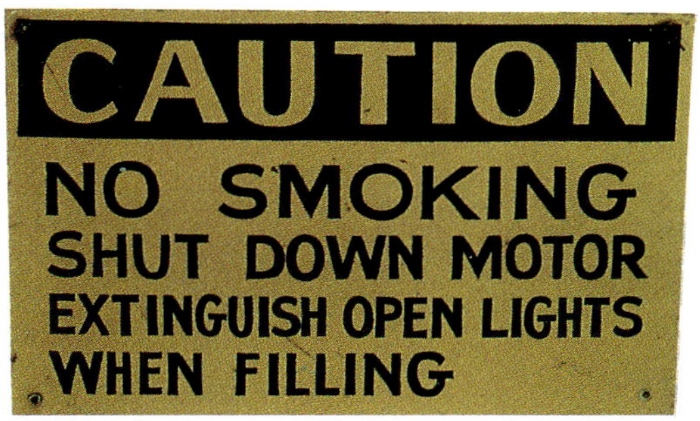

This is an extremely early fire-hazard sign, used 1916-1920. Note the reference to "lamps burning," indicating a motorist was to extinguish acetylene headlamps or running lamps prior to fueling. $200-$250. *Jackie Knott Collection.*

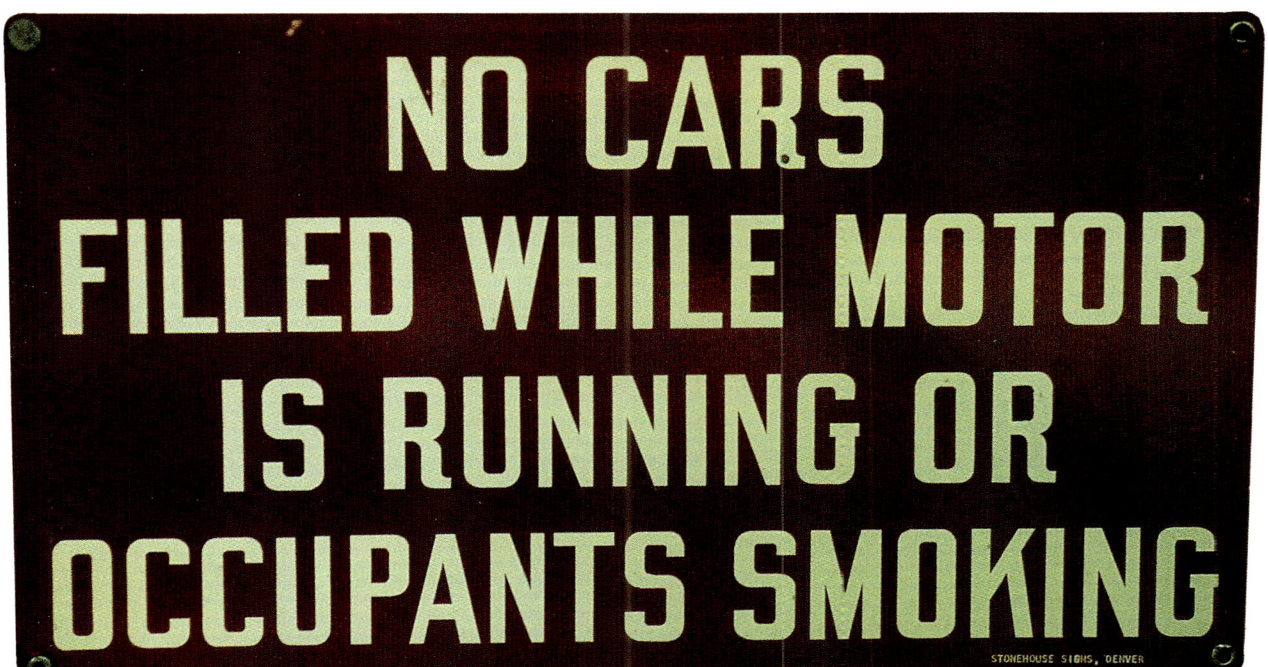

Another porcelain example of a Sinclair safety warning sign $200-$250.
Jackie Knott Collection.

These one-gallon motor oil cans are representative of those used 1916-1926. $175-$275. *Jackie Knott Collection.*

These Sinclair cans are typical of those used in the 1916-1920 era. No Listing. *Jackie Knott Collection.*

Shown here are several examples of early Sinclair globes of assorted uses. The globe on the far right is Sinclair's first gas pump globe, used 1916-1918, and is valued at $1200. The others are of uncertain usage and date from the 1926-1930 era. *Jackie Knott Collection.*

This 8" x 20" tin-litho sign advertises Opaline Motor Oil in the era (prior to 1916) that Opaline was a Cudahy Oil Company trademark. $400. *Jackie Knott Collection.*

Brass stencils were used to imprint product drums, cans, and other containers. $25-$100.
Jackie Knott Collection.

Earliest Sinclair delivery vehicles were painted white. This tank wagon dates from the 1916-1920 era. No Listing. *Jackie Knott Collection.*

One of the earliest known photos of a Sinclair station is this station, photographed in an unknown location about 1919. *Scott Benjamin Collection.*

Innovative Marketing & "H-C"

As the 1920s began, Sinclair took its rightful place alongside other major oil companies, a new generation of enterprises that did not trace their origin to Standard. Unshackled by history and an "we've always done it that way" attitude, Sinclair began to innovate.

Initially, to expand marketing facilities, operations that already included terminals, bulk plants, and filling stations had been purchased. Concentration was initially in urban markets, as stations were added in New York and various cities in New England through the purchase of Keith Oil Company of Triverton, Rhode Island. In Detroit, Central Oil and Gasoline was purchased and their nearly twenty stations were rebranded Sinco. Other independents were added in upstate New York, throughout Ohio, and in the Midwest.

It was in Chicago, however, that Sinclair innovation truly did shine. Here, beginning with a single station ringed with curb pumps and not at all unlike Gulf's first-ever station in Pittsburgh, Sinclair developed the concept of neighborhood "filling stations" situated among "greasing palaces" that catered to areas served by perhaps a dozen smaller stations. While the development of service-oriented stations selling tires, batteries, and accessories ("TBA") is generally credited to innovative marketer Colonial Beacon in the Boston area, Sinclair was operating its "greasing palaces," specializing in automotive service and TBA sales over five years before Colonial Beacon. In the years before 1930, the "greasing palace" concept was spread to many of Sinclair's urban markets. Sinclair also did quite well out in the country. They were among the first to market through wholesale "jobbers" and commission agents. Through those agents, as it remains to this day, Sinclair gasoline was sold in rural areas, locations that could not have proved profitable if company-direct operation had been specified. Sinclair signs hung in front of country stores in every state from the Atlantic Coast to the Rocky Mountains by 1930. Also during this era Sinclair began marketing that was specifically aimed at the agricultural industry. Farm shows were promoted, farm literature was available, and a complete line of farm products were developed, sold through jobbers, agents, and their dealers, as well as many other "nontraditional" dealers, such as farm agents that did not sell other petroleum products. Among the best known Sinclair farm products was Sinclair P.D. Stock Spray, well respected by farmers throughout the nation.

Advances in automotive engine design had seen major steps forward during the decade of 1910-1920. Early two-cylinder and four-

Curb sign and stand advertising Sinclair Gasoline, as was used for identification at curb pumps and other locations where Sinclair products were sold, used from 1920 until the early 1930s. $600-$700. *Jackie Knott Collection.*

Sinclair stations of the 1920s often were flanked by wooden fences. Advertising signs for Sinclair lubricants were attached to these fences, including this wood-framed tin-litho Sinclair Mobiline used from 1928-1932.
When Socony and Vacuum merged in 1931, adopting the Mobil trademarks nationwide, trademark infringement laws prevented Sinclair from continuing the use of the trademark Mobiline. Sinclair Pennsylvania was introduced in 1931 to replace Sinclair Mobiline. $350-$500. *Jackie Knott Collection.*

cylinder designs gradually gave way to six-cylinder in-line engines. As early as 1915 Cadillac offered a V-8 engine in certain models. Engine development, however, was hampered by the lack of availability of higher octane motor fuels necessary in developing higher compression ratios. The petroleum industry experimented with a number of blends and additives to gasoline in an attempt to create a fuel of higher anti-knock capability. Of the early additives, a blend of benzene and gasoline marketed as "BENZOL" offered the most promise. At Sinclair's earliest stations, the single motor fuel sold was known simply as Sinclair Sinco Gasoline. The first effort by a major gasoline marketer to introduce a higher octane gasoline came in 1922 when Standard Of Indiana introduced "Solite," a gasoline with higher specific gravity (the method for determining octane rating was not established until 1929) than Standard's "Red Crown." Also in 1922 Sinclair began offering Sinclair "Special" Gasoline. In many markets Sinclair offered Sinclair Benzol Motor Fuel, a benzol-gasoline premium blend, which led to the introduction of Sinclair Aircraft. Never intended as a fuel for airplanes, but rather an automotive fuel that was truly of aviation quality, Sinclair's benzol premium was renamed Sinclair Aircraft about 1926.

One of many posters used over the years advertising Sinclair products. $150-$200. *Jackie Knott Collection.*

In early 1923, the General Motors Research Labs at Dayton, Ohio, began testing the addition of tetraethyl lead to gasoline. Marketing experimentation began when GM teamed with Dayton independent Refiners Oil Company to introduce an "ethylized" gas, blending tetraethyl lead with gasoline at the pump. The experiment was quite successful and in September 1923 GM teamed up with Standard of Indiana to introduce Ethyl gasoline on a large scale. The following August GM and Standard Oil of New Jersey formed Ethyl Gasoline Corporation to franchise the Ethyl additive to gasoline marketers worldwide. The ink had hardly dried on this agreement when lead poisoning deaths in the Ethyl plants brought about a moratorium of the sale of "ethylized" gasoline until further study of potential harmful effects could be determined. After over a year of study by the US Surgeon General, Ethyl gasoline was reintroduced, with some restrictions on handling of the tetraethyl lead additive. With the re-introduction of Ethyl, every refiner meeting the Ethyl franchise requirements quickly signed on. Those who were deemed ineligible, for one reason or another, quickly introduced their own premium grade products in order to compete with Ethyl. Thus, in a period of about two years, virtually every marketer began offering at least two grades of gasoline. Sinclair was among those few marketers that had been unable to secure an Ethyl franchise, so in 1926 Sinclair introduced a fuel whose name would become synonymous with the corporate name over the next thirty-five years.

Sinclair one-gallon cans from the 1920s. $25-$100. *Jackie Knott Collection.*

To the research and development people, and to the refinery personnel, Sinclair's new product was known as "Houston Concentrate," named for their additive package developed first at Houston. To the marketing people, however, the standard abbreviation for the new product, "H-C," was said to mean "High Compression." With this development, Sinclair HC Gasoline was first offered in Chicago in the summer of 1926. Those marketers that had, prior to the introduction of Ethyl, offered a premium grade product—possibly a benzol blend or an "aviation" grade (aviation being a common trade name for these non-ethyl premiums in the 1920s)—often continued to market this product alongside their new "Ethyl" or other leaded premium. Sinclair was no exception, and continued to market Sinclair Aircraft alongside Sinclair Gasoline (regular) and Sinclair HC (premium) into the early 1930s.

Ethyl Gasoline Corporation standards required that no marketer add tetraethyl lead to any product that did not meet certain quality standards. Likewise, no marketer could offer an Ethyl fuel as anything other than a premium grade...specifically, tetraethyl lead could not be added to any approved refiner's regular grade product until the terms of the Ethyl franchise agreement were modified in 1933. Sinclair finally did receive Ethyl approval in 1931, and replaced Sinclair HC gasoline with Sinclair HC with Ethyl. This arrangement survived just a year or so when Sinclair Ethyl was introduced as the company's premium grade product. Sinclair HC, remaining "leaded" but no longer billed as an "Ethyl" grade, became the company's regular grade product. It was a product mix that would serve the company well during the depression years.

This porcelain sign was used on oil cabinets in the early 1920s. $400-$600. *Jackie Knott Collection.*

Double sided porcelain Sinclair Gasoline 24" curb sign from the 1920-1935 era. $400-$500. *Jackie Knott Collection.*

Double sided porcelain Sinclair Gasoline 30" curb sign from the 1920-1935 era. $400-$500. *Jackie Knott Collection.*

Double sided porcelain Sinclair Oils 30" curb sign from the 1920-1935 era. $400-$500. *Jackie Knott Collection.*

These chalk bears reminded customers to "Bear in mind Sinclair Oils." $200. *Jackie Knott Collection.*

This porcelain Opaline Motor Oil sign was used in the early 1920s. $350-$400. *Jackie Knott Collection.*

This tin litho sign shows an early 1920s Sinclair Opaline gallon can. $450. *Jackie Knott Collection.*

This restored wheel-cart oil lubester dates from the 1920s and displays signage from that era.
$2000-$2500. *Jackie Knott Collection.*

Packaged motor oils and lubricants were sold from these Sinclair branded oil carts in the early 1920s. $1000-$1500. *Jackie Knott Collection.*

Curb sign and stand advertising Sinclair HC Gasoline, as was used for identification at curb pumps and other locations where Sinclair products were sold, used from 1926 until the early 1940s. $600-$800. *Jackie Knott Collection.*

Model T Fords required special motor oils to eliminate engine noises. This sign advertises Sinclair Opaline "F", made specifically for Ford automobiles, and dates from the early 1920s. $650. *Jackie Knott Collection.*

Sinclair Oils facilities identification sign from the early 1920s. Approximately 14" by 8', but other sizes are known, as are signs with white letters on a green background. $450-$500. *Jackie Knott Collection.*

This tin-litho flange sign advertises Sinclair Opaline motor oil and displays a can from the early 1920s. No listing. *Jackie Knott Collection.*

Flange signs often identified garages, grocery stores, and other locations offering Sinclair products. These tin litho signs are from the early 1920s and measure approximately 18" in diameter. $250-$400. *Jackie Knott Collection.*

Sinclair Gasoline dealer identification sign from the early 1920s. While this example has a green border, examples are known with a red border as well. $400-$500. *Jackie Knott Collection.*

Shown here is an example of a Sinclair Oils one-piece etched globe in the 12" diameter narrow-body format. No listing. *Jackie Knott Collection.*

Sinclair was finally granted an Ethyl franchise in 1932, and numerous variations of Sinclair Ethyl globes are known. This one differs from the others in that the lettering is not outlined. $750. *Jackie Knott Collection.*

Shown here is an example of a Sinclair Oils one-piece etched-finish globe in the 12" diameter wide-body format. No listing. *Jackie Knott Collection.*

Okaw Valley Oil Company branded Sinclair globe. This is an example of a globe from an independent jobber who was in the process of branding Sinclair, probably in the early 1920s. No listing. *Jackie Knott Collection.*

In the late 1920s vertical signage was introduced for attachment to station canopy columns. This signage advertised Sinclair's various motor oil products. Shown here are examples of signage for Sinclair Opaline and Mobiline and Mobiline's replacement, Pennsylvania. These signs are all known in both flat and embossed versions. $350 each. *Jackie Knott Collection.*

An early three-gallon Sinclair transformer oil container. $150. *Jackie Knott Collection.*

An early Sinclair branded funnel. $35. *Jackie Knott Collection.*

On the left is a Sinclair Opaline can from the 1920s, and on the right is a Stock Spray can from the 1940s. $50-$75. *Jackie Knott Collection.*

Early drum-type oil cans, originally storage for Pierce Pennant Motor Oil and Sinclair Opaline Motor Oil. $250-$350. *Jackie Knott Collection.*

More drum-type cans. Sinclair Pennsylvania (left) replaced Sinclair Mobiline (right) in 1931. $250-$350. *Jackie Knott Collection.*

Several Sinclair five-gallon cans, imprinted for transmission lubricants. $25-$100. *Jackie Knott Collection.*

This 8" diameter porcelain sign with mounting tab was designed for use on motor oil lubesters and dates from the 1920s. $450. *Jackie Knott Collection.*

This photo shows the Sinclair Gasoline 24" curb sign in close view. Curb signs are among the most popular items with collectors today. $400-$500. *Jackie Knott Collection.*

Another design of 8" diameter porcelain sign with mounting tab was designed for use on motor oil lubesters and dates from the 1920s. $450. *Jackie Knott Collection.*

Cast frames holding price and calculation cards were mounted on cylinder support rods on visible pumps. This frame displays the Sinclair trademark along the outer edge. $75. *Jackie Knott Collection.*

Wooden rules and other measuring sticks all bear various Sinclair trademarks. $10-$50. *Jackie Knott Collection.*

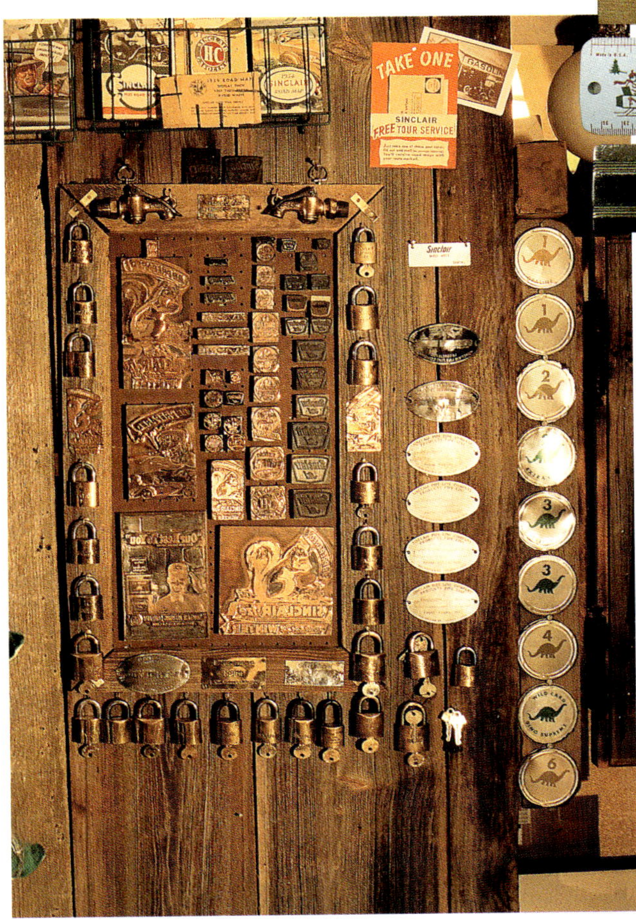

Embossed padlocks were used to secure company property, and printer's type-blocks were used by letterpress printers to incorporate Sinclair graphics into printed material. $25-$100. *Jackie Knott Collection.*

This 48" porcelain sign advertises Sinclair's benzol-premium "Aircraft" gasoline. It dates from 1927. $3500. *Jackie Knott Collection.*

These measuring cans were used to transfer Sinclair products among various points of bulk storage. $50. *Jackie Knott Collection.*

One-piece etched Sinclair Oils globe, used from the early 1920s until after 1927 when a baked-finish globe was introduced. $1300. *Scott Benjamin Collection.*

One-piece baked finish Sinclair Oils globe, used from 1926 until the early 1930s. $1500. *Scott Benjamin Collection.*

An unusual retrofit metal band globe displaying Sinclair Oils lenses and dating from the late 1920s. Sinclair never specified the use of metal frame globes, but in some cases where jobbers selling other brands had metal-frame bodies in place and converted to the Sinclair brand, special lenses were made to be installed at existing locations. $2000. *Scott Benjamin Collection.*

In parts of the south, Sinclair's motor grade gasoline was branded Sinclair Pennant, a name Sinclair inherited with the purchase of Pierce Petroleum. Shown here is a Pennant globe from the 1930s. $750. *Scott Benjamin Collection.*

From 1916 until 1934, Sinclair's regular grade motor fuel was branded simply "Sinclair Gasoline." This one-piece etched globe dates from the 1920-1927 era. $1000. *Scott Benjamin Collection.*

The earliest globe to display the familiar Sinclair HC logo is this one-piece etched version manufactured in 1926. $1250. *Scott Benjamin Collection.*

Another unusual retrofit metal band globe displaying Sinclair HC lenses and dating from the late 1920s. $1800. *Scott Benjamin Collection.*

A one-piece baked finish Sinclair HC globe was specified for new locations in the 1927-1931 era. $950. *Scott Benjamin Collection.*

This early and very generic one-piece etched "Benzol Motor Fuel" globe was one of the first globes used to advertise Sinclair's Benzol grade fuel. It has been confirmed as Sinclair from early photos. $2500. *Scott Benjamin Collection.*

Sinclair's first Ethyl product was aptly branded Sinclair HC with Ethyl. In 1934 Sinclair HC became a regular grade and Sinclair Ethyl was introduced. This three-piece glass globe was used in the 1934-1942, with similar versions known without outlines around the "Sinclair" lettering and with the later (1942-1947) "Ethyl Corporation" banner across the Ethyl logo. $650. *Scott Benjamin Collection.*

When one-piece baked finish globes were introduced in 1927, the Sinclair Aircraft logo was revised to primarily red, with dark green outlines. $3500. *Scott Benjamin Collection.*

In 1926 Sinclair's benzol-grade fuel was renamed Sinclair Aircraft. Shown here is an early one-piece etched globe. $4500. *Scott Benjamin Collection.*

Here is an example of collector ingenuity. This one-piece Sinclair Aircraft globe was custom painted in this very attractive color scheme. While we never recommend this practice, this particular globe stands out as one-of-a kind artwork. No Listing. *Scott Benjamin Collection.*

Among the rarest and most beautiful of all Sinclair signs is the red, white, and green Sinclair Aircraft sign used in the late 1920s. $3500.

The third version of the 48" Sinclair Aircraft porcelain sign, primarily red with green outlines. $2500.

This early Sinclair station was selling Sinclair's benzol grade fuel about 1921. *Courtesy of Erwin Schmidt.*

This spectacular wood-framed sign advertises Sinclair Pennsylvania Motor Oil, a brand new product (having replaced Mobiline) when this sign first appeared in 1931. $750-$1000. *Jackie Knott Collection.*

This Sinclair bulk plant from the late 1920s is typical of Sinclair plants nationwide during that time. Painted bulk tanks advertise Sinclair products.

Sinclair's first corporate owned stations were known as "Greasing Palaces." Here are two shots of Sinclair's Kansas City location #3, taken about 1927 and again about 1930.

Des-Andy Oil Company was an early Michigan Sinclair distributor. They were operating this station, believed to be in the Detroit suburbs, about 1922.

Sinclair gasoline was dispensed from Fry "Mae West" pumps when this picture was taken in Phoebus, Virginia, about 1925.

Sinclair Foreign Marketing

Although Sinclair is generally considered to be a domestic company, during the 1920s the growing markets in Europe caught their attention, and an investment was made in distribution facilities and marketing in Belgium, England, Holland, and other parts of northern Europe. Some crude oil exploration in Europe was also attempted, but to no avail. As automobile ownership increased in Europe, Sinclair's marketing presence grew, and their motor oils and other lubricants were of particular interest to the customer base in these countries, as Sinclair Oils were often considered to be far superior to those marketed by locally owned and operated companies. Sinclair would continue to operate in Europe until the eve of World War II, when, sensing the upcoming turmoil, they sold out their operations, abandoning any attempt to market in Europe until after World War II when importers again returned Sinclair's high quality lubricants to select European markets.

Other foreign marketing can hardly be considered "foreign," since their extensive Mexican presence was little more than an extension of Pierce Petroleum's existing base in the south central United States. Pierce's Productos Sinclair "Red Rooster" signs were displayed in Mexico until all outside petroleum marketing was expropriated by Mexico in 1938. Cuba was a strong Sinclair market, and remained so until the advent of Castro's communism drove foreign investments from the country in 1959.

Oddly enough, Sinclair apparently never marketed in Canada. During the extensive research that preceded this work, the question why came up numerous times. All

Sinclair was active in foreign markets, particularly in Mexico after the purchase of Pierce Petroleum. The "Productos Sinclair" sign was used in Mexico from 1930-1938 and is a highly sought-after sign today. $1500-$2000. *Jackie Knott Collection.*

that can be confirmed is that Sinclair had exploration and production properties in western Canada in the 1950s and 1960s, and that it is possible they owned a minority interest in Canada's Supertest Petroleum during the 1950s. If anyone can provide further information on any Sinclair marketing in Canada, please contact the authors.

Sinclair products were distributed in Mexico through a subsidiary, Pierce Oil Company, S. A. This road map shows the Pierce "Productos Sinclair" imaging and dates from about 1930. No Listing. *Wayne Henderson Collection.*

Sinclair's conversion of the former Pierce Petroleum marketing properties in Mexico introduced the Productos Sinclair (Sinclair Products) trademark throughout Mexico in the 1930s. Shown here is a road map from the early 1930s. No listing. *Jackie Knott Collection.*

This porcelain sign was used in Sinclair's European marketing, primarily in Belgium, prior to World War II. $650. *Jackie Knott Collection.*

Growth Through Acquisition

In our book *Standard Oil The First 125 Years*, the Standard Oil Company, Rockefeller's Standard, was looked on as an "Angel of Mercy" to the infant petroleum industry. During the Great Depression, however, it was Sinclair that proved to be the "Angel of Mercy" to many regional oil companies.

Standard had a hand in their position, however, for it was Standard Oil Company of Indiana that financed much of Sinclair's stability and growth during the depression. While that seems like quite an unusual statement, it was Standard's purchase of Sinclair's pipe line operation and a large portion of their crude exploration operations that financed Sinclair throughout the depression.

This die-cut standup from the 1930s advertises Sinclair Opaline Motor Oil. $500. *Jackie Knott Collection.*

Many years earlier alliances had been formed between Sinclair and Standard (Indiana). Standard had purchased a partial interest in Sinclair Pipe Line Company in the early 1920s. The move was a logical one, since the pipeline led to Sinclair's East Chicago facility, abutting Standard's Whiting Refinery. Crude gathered throughout the mid-continent was piped to the neighboring complexes. Sinclair's involvement with Standard was not limited to pipelines, however, as both were involved in the attempted purchase and development of the government's crude reserves at a facility known as Teapot Dome in Wyoming. Sinclair Consolidated and Standard were partners in Mammoth Oil Company, an entity created for the development of the Teapot Dome reserves. The Sinclair Pipe Line Company, owned by both Sinclair and Standard, expanded westward to serve the development. And likewise when the Teapot Dome sale was invalidated by the courts, both Sinclair and Standard saw significant loss of their investment. With this kind of interaction, the sale of the remaining interest in the pipe line operation seemed only logical.

In retrospect, Harry Sinclair saw the depression for what it really proved to be. While the pipeline (along with a portion of Sinclair crude

This porcelain die-cut dinosaur was used in secondary signage that was attached to station identification sign poles. Other examples were made of wood or plastic and painted green or white. Porcelain or wood, $500; plastic, $150. *Jackie Knott Collection.*

production that Standard had also purchased) would have proved valuable to the growth-minded organization, Sinclair saw, correctly, that what would be necessary to survive this depression, worse than earlier recessions, was cash. With the sale, Sinclair Consolidated, which became simply "Consolidated Oil Corporation" in 1932, had the cash that was necessary to continue to operate and grow in the economic conditions existing in the early years of the Depression. Cash in hand, Harry Sinclair went shopping.

Sinclair stations of the 1930s often were flanked by wooden fences. Advertising signs for Sinclair lubricants were attached to these fences, including this framed composite-board Sinclair Pennsylvania sign used from 1934-1936. $600. *Jackie Knott Collection.*

First on the shopping list was Pierce Petroleum. Pierce, formerly Waters-Pierce, was based in St. Louis and was one of the thirty-three surviving companies dispersed at the breakup of Standard Oil in 1911. Pierce marketed under the Pennant brand in the south-central United States and throughout Mexico. Sinclair purchased Pierce in 1930, and former Pennant stations in this country were re-branded Sinclair within a year or so. In Mexico, however, the marketing organization Pierce Oil Company, S.A., was maintained intact and Pierce service stations in Mexico displayed the sign "Productos Sinclair" (*Sinclair Products*) featuring a large red rooster, until Mexico expropriated foreign oil company holdings in 1938.

Another Standard sibling was next on the list. In 1932 Sinclair purchased Prairie Oil and Gas of Independence, Kansas. Prairie was exclusively a production and pipeline operation, and in one fell swoop Sinclair regained a large portion of that which had been sold to Standard. Although Prairie did not market gasoline and oils, the company had earlier acquired a 65% interest in Producers and Refiners Corporation, better known as Parco, which operated a refinery at Parco,

Wyoming, and marketed gasoline in Wyoming, Idaho, and Utah. Prairie had acquired its interest in Parco largely thorough default, and shortly after Sinclair purchased Prairie, Parco was bankrupt. In 1934 Sinclair, already a majority creditor to Parco, salvaged most of Parco's desirable assets, integrating them into Sinclair's existing operations.

While most of Sinclair's growth and acquisition interest had been in the mid-continent area, their interest expanded in 1932 to the West Coast with the purchase of California's Rio Grande Oil Company. Largely a marketing firm, Rio Grande contributed some production to Sinclair's existing operations. Service stations in California retained the Rio Grande brand name, although Sinclair lubricants would be offered through the existing outlets for many years to come.

This older, 1930-1934, Sinclair Opaline fence sign is made of wood framed tin $450. *Jackie Knott Collection.*

The largest of the Depression-era purchases was Richfield. Richfield Oil Company of California had been founded in 1901 and became a flamboyant marketer during the 1920s. A network of service stations up and down the West Coast was established, and in 1929 Richfield entered eastern markets with the purchase of New York's Walburn Oil Company. From Walburn's holdings, Richfield Oil Company of New York was established and a jobber network all along the Atlantic coast was solicited. Unchecked expansion met with the Great Depression, and by 1931, Richfield was bankrupt. Sinclair purchased Richfield Oil Company of New York outright in 1935, and in 1936 Sinclair, using assets acquired with Rio Grande Oil Company, participated in the reorganization of Richfield. A new Richfield Oil Corporation was formed in 1937, with Sinclair and Cities Service as owners. With the creation of this entity, Richfield Oil Corporation again became a thriving operation, branding stations under the Richfield and Rio Grande names throughout the west. Richfield would reappear in Sinclair's history over thirty years later when, merged with Atlantic Refining to form Atlantic Richfield, they would purchase and for a time operate Sinclair.

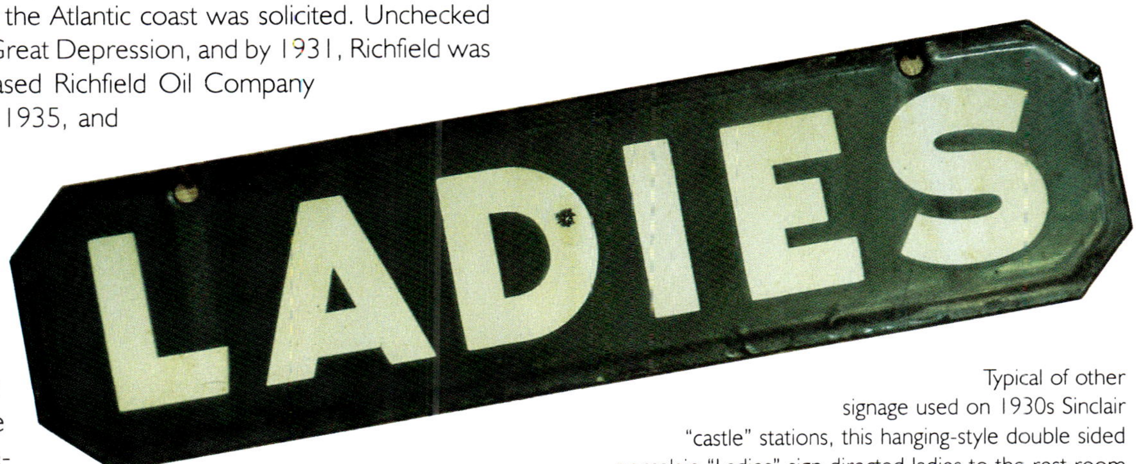

Typical of other signage used on 1930s Sinclair "castle" stations, this hanging-style double sided porcelain "Ladies" sign directed ladies to the rest room entrance around on the side of the station. $75-$100. *Jackie Knott Collection.*

The Richfield purchase was Sinclair's final expansion prior to World War II. By the mid-1930s better financial times were returning for many businesses and it is unlikely, looking back, that Sinclair management found many more opportunities like those they had taken advantage of in the early 1930s. Europe was beginning to see some of

This porcelain sign was displayed adjacent to Sinclair pump islands in the 1930s, directing motorists not to smoke near the pumps. $250. *Jackie Knott Collection.*

the turmoil that would lead to the War, and in the later 1930s Sinclair management began looking for ways to minimize their exposure. By 1941 all of Sinclair's European operations had been sold off, resulting in no loss through expropriation during World War II. Refinery research departments were concentrating on methods to manufacture higher octane gasolines, some of which was already being offered to an ever growing aviation market. Aviation gasoline would prove to be the commodity that would win (or lose) the war.

During the 1930s Sinclair stations that accepted the proprietary Sinclair credit card displayed this sign for the convenience of passing motorists. Not all stations carrying a particular gasoline brand were required to accept their credit cards! $200. *Jackie Knott Collection.*

Also in those years prior to 1940, domestic marketing was upgraded, as many new service station sites were selected. A new station prototype, commonly referred to as the Sinclair "Castle" was developed in the early 1930s, and hundreds were built along major highways. The new stations consolidated the array of services and products formerly offered only at Sinclair's "Greasing Palaces" in major markets, making the neighborhood, small town, or highway station a complete "service station" with a full line of TBA (Tires, Batteries, Accessories) products. Although many would see lean years during the war, with gas and tire rationing devastating these high-margin items, Sinclair's station network was truly completed by the late 1930s and Sinclair signs were seen in all states east of the Rocky Mountains.

These porcelain rest room signs date from the early 1940s and reference a sanitation procedure that used ultraviolet light to kill germs in Sinclair rest rooms. $350-$450 on die-cut sign, $100 each on rest room identification signs. *Jackie Knott Collection.*

This porcelain sign advertised Sinclair battery charging service in the early 1930s. $400-$500. *Jackie Knott Collection.*

Sinclair's premium-grade motor oil, Sinclair Pennsylvania, is advertised on this 11" diameter porcelain sign designed to attach to lubester tanks. This version was used 1936 through 1946, and oil cans of the era match this design. Larger versions of this sign, a 16" sign used on trucks, and a 24" sign used as a curb sign, complete on of the most sought-after sets of Sinclair signage. 11", $800; 16", $1200; 24", $1600. *Jackie Knott Collection.*

Sinclair's regular-grade motor oil, Sinclair Opaline, is advertised on this 11" diameter porcelain sign designed to attach to lubester tanks. This version was used from 1936 through 1946, and oil cans of the era match this design. Larger versions of this sign, a 16" sign used on trucks, and a 24" sign used as a curb sign, complete one of the most sought-after sets of Sinclair signage. 11", $800; 16", $1200; 24", $1600. *Jackie Knott Collection.*

Shown in this photo is a Sinclair "Indexed Lubrication" sign used in the service-bay area in the 1930s, $350; as well as a 1960s dual Sinclair-Goodyear sign, $150. *Jackie Knott Collection.*

Sinclair's branded fuel oil program for jobbers and other distributors was trademarked "Super Flame," as was their kerosene product. This sign advertised Super Flame kerosene in the 1930s. $400-$500. *Jackie Knott Collection.*

Over the years Sinclair used various credit card acceptance signs, many of which are shown throughout this book. This, however, is perhaps the best known. Seen here complete with the accenting die-cut dinosaur, these signs attached to identification sign poles in the late 1930s and early 1940s. $700-$1000, complete. *Jackie Knott Collection.*

Curb sign and stand advertising Sinclair Opaline Motor Oil, displaying the logo used 1936-1946. $1500-$1800. *Jackie Knott Collection.*

Sinclair cans from the 1930s, shown here as a pitcher and cup set. *Jackie Knott Collection.*

Curb sign and stand advertising Sinclair HC Gasoline and Sinclair Super Flame heating oil. Used as secondary signage at bulk facilities. $600-$800. *Jackie Knott Collection.*

Curb sign and stand advertising Sinclair Opaline Motor Oil, displaying the logo used 1932-1936. $700-$800. *Jackie Knott Collection.*

Sinclair agricultural products included P.D. Stock Spray. These pump sprayers were used for applying P.D. Stock Spray. $25-$100. *Jackie Knott Collection.*

Various containers for Sinclair P.D. Stock Spray. $25-$100. *Jackie Knott Collection.*

Assorted Sinclair quart cans. Cans on the far left of the top and bottom rows were used 1934-1936. The top right can dates from the 1920s, and the rest were used from 1936-1946. $50-$150. *Jackie Knott Collection.*

Sinclair Stock Spray cans from the 1930s and 1940s. $25-$100. *Jackie Knott Collection.*

Sinclair was one of the first companies to standardize their station signage. These porcelain signs were used on both proprietary-design stations and dealer sites of any design. The "Washing" and "Lubrication" signs are 9" x 7', while the "Sinclair" panel is 14" x 8'. $100-$350. *Jackie Knott Collection.*

Shown here is a Sinclair Gasoline globe decaled for the 1930s motor-grade product "Green." Such temporary grade identification is not unusual. $650. *Jackie Knott Collection.*

In the early 1930s, as Sinclair was evolving from using one-piece glass globes to three-piece glass globes, they experimented with using pump door decals on glass bodies intended for use with glass lenses. Improper illumination, as is shown here, brought about a swift conversion to normal three-piece globes, but not before examples of every grade globe was created. Shown here is the regular-grade Sinclair Gasoline decaled globe. $450. *Jackie Knott Collection.*

Sinclair marketed their motor-grade (economy) motor fuel under several different trademarks during the early 1930s. In parts of the south, the product was known as Sinclair Green Gasoline. This is an extremely rare globe. No Listing. *Jackie Knott Collection.*

Standardized station identification signage in use from the late 1920s until the end of World War II. This example is 12" x 84", one of numerous sizes known to exist. $500. *Jackie Knott Collection.*

This fold up poster shows the proper installation arrangement for Sinclair signage. Measuring 60" x 120", is accurately reproduces the Sinclair "castle" station design used during the 1930s. No listing. *Jackie Knott Collection.*

During World War II, Sinclair Opaline Motor Oil was sold from branded bottles like the one shown here. $75. *Jackie Knott Collection.*

Shown here are desk clocks typical of those used by Sinclair executives. $25-$100. *Jackie Knott Collection.*

These photos show official Sinclair attendant hats. Notice the evolution of logos through the years. $75-$150. *Jackie Knott Collection.*

Various road maps
from the 1930s are framed in a Sinclair refinery
safety poster frame. $100. *Jackie Knott Collection.*

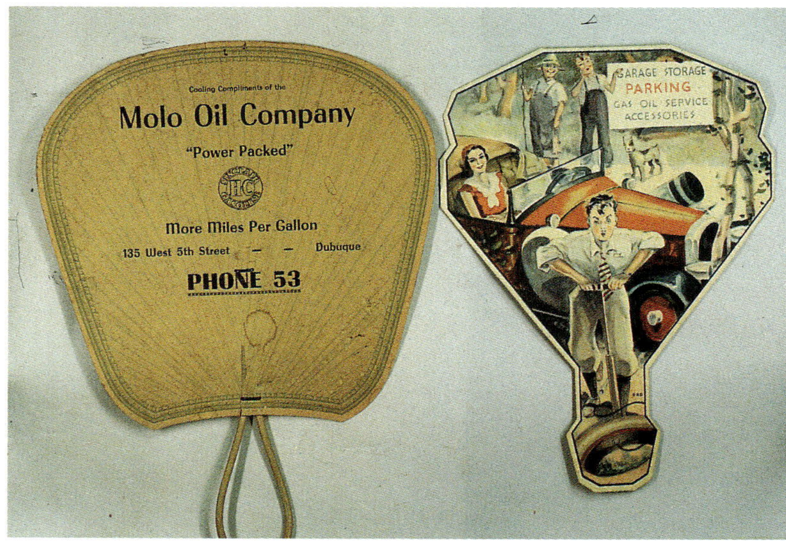

Molo Oil Company, the Sinclair marketer in Dubuque, Iowa, and surrounding areas, used these fans for promoting Sinclair products. $25-$100. *Jackie Knott Collection.*

Several Sinclair "lubrication caps" $25-$100. *Jackie Knott Collection.*

Shown here is an assortment of road maps from the 1930s, displayed in a 1961 road map rack. $25-$100. *Jackie Knott Collection.*

Assorted Sinclair cans are displayed on an oil can rack from the 1930s that includes a chart to help in selecting the proper grade of motor oil for your car. $25-$100. *Jackie Knott Collection.*

Shown here are several gas pump ad glasses from the 1930s. $25-$100. *Jackie Knott Collection.*

Among the rarest of all ad glasses are these from the early 1930s, including a Sinclair Green (motor grade product in southeastern states) glass and a Sinclair US Motor Specification glass. $25-$100. *Jackie Knott Collection.*

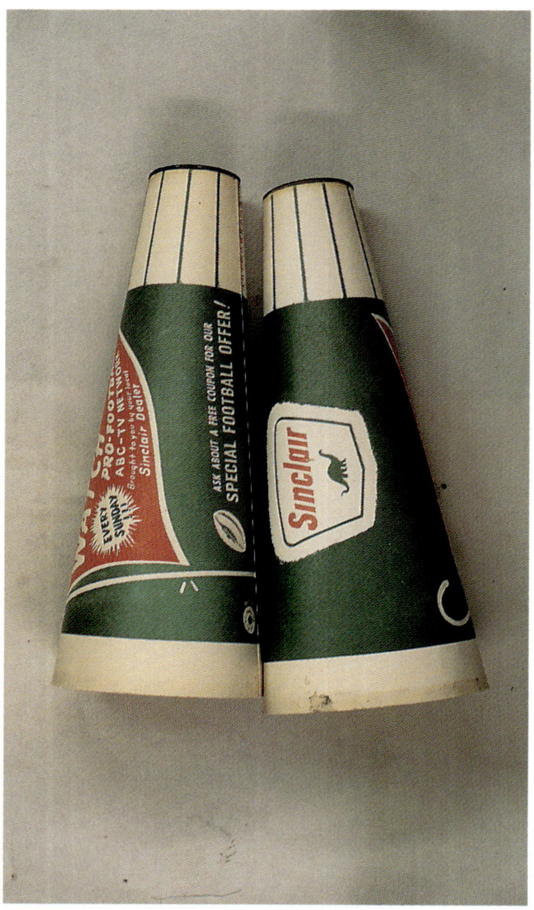

Sinclair promotional megaphones. $25. *Jackie Knott Collection.*

This promotional folder from the early 1930s advertises Sinclair lubrication services. $50.
Jackie Knott Collection.

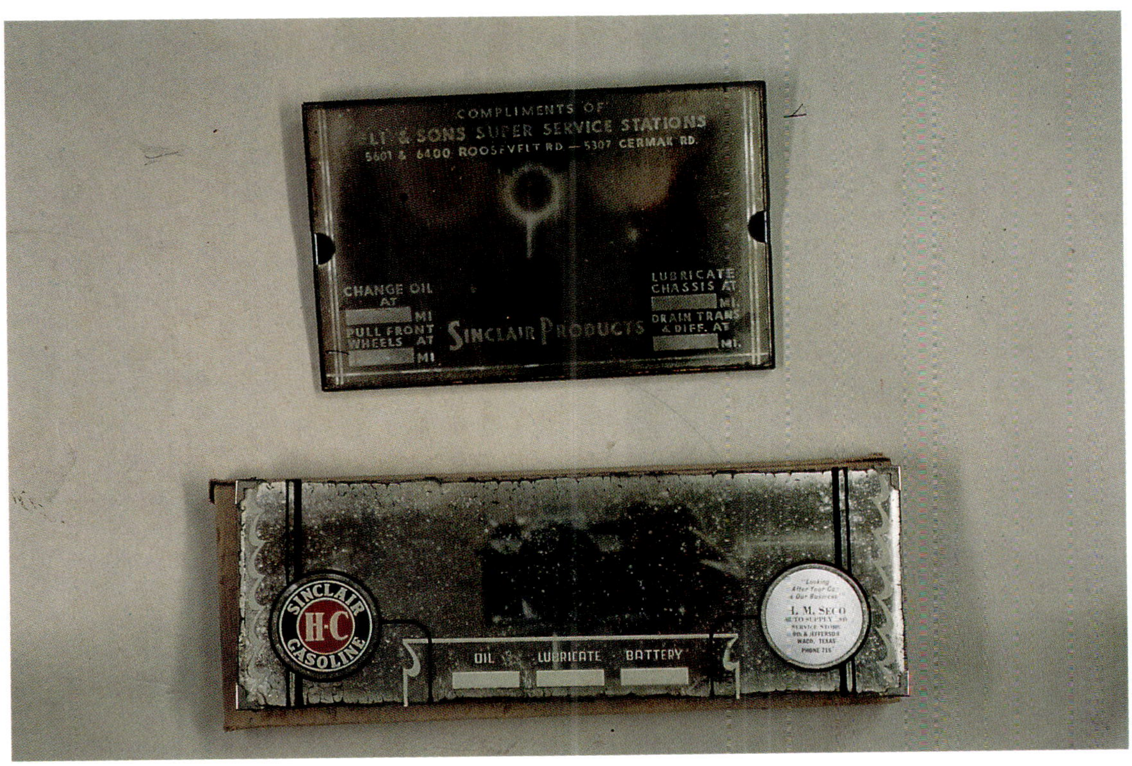

Oil change reminders used by Sinclair dealers in the 1930s. $25.
Jackie Knott Collection.

Sinclair, well known in rural markets, offered an entire range of products specifically for agricultural use which were advertised through these various publications, aimed at the farm trade. $25. *Jackie Knott Collection.*

Sinclair was one of the few marketers to develop an image for tractor fuel, a blend that was usually 90% kerosene mixed with 10% gasoline. This logo was developed to advertise a broad range of Sinclair agricultural products, and is known to exist on an extremely rare globe that was displayed atop pumps dispensing tractor fuel. *Jackie Knott Collection.*

Sinclair road maps of the 1930s, displayed in a 1950s road map rack. $25-$100. *Jackie Knott Collection.*

Sinclair, with nationwide marketing almost from the start, was among the first marketers to use proprietary credit cards as a selling tool. This acceptance sign dates from the early 1930s. $250. *Jackie Knott Collection.*

Sinclair motor oils were offered from bulk in these branded five gallon containers. The logos shown match the sealed quart cans of the 1934-1936 era. $50 each. *Jackie Knott Collection.*

So-called "pinback" buttons have advertised Sinclair products throughout the twentieth century. $25-$100. *Jackie Knott Collection.*

Sinclair keychains and other jewelry with Sinclair trademarks through the years. $25-$100. *Jackie Knott Collection.*

Sinclair used various sports-related advertising campaigns in the 1930s, 40s, and 50s. *Jackie Knott Collection.* This Sinclair baseball is signed by Babe Ruth, and is part of a 1930s promotion. $10-$50. *Jackie Knott Collection.*

A Sinclair industrial product, Gascon, is advertised on this clock. No listing. *Jackie Knott Collection.*

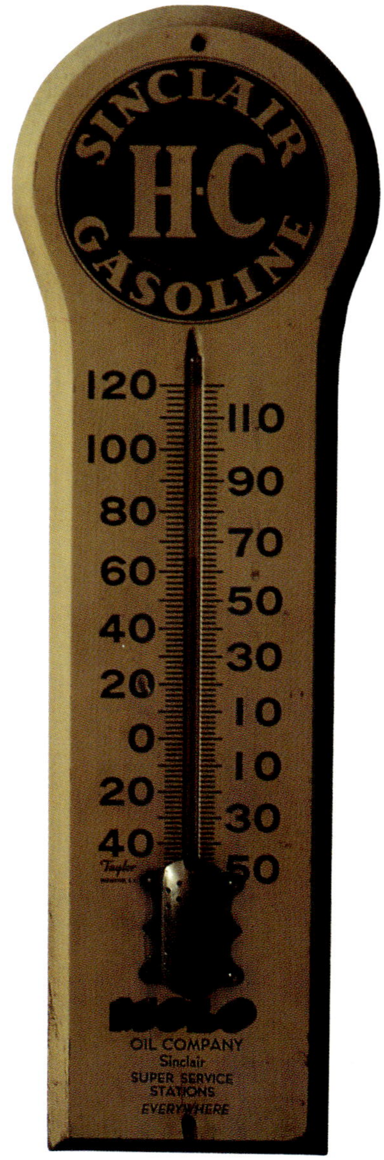

This wooden thermometer from the 1930s advertises Sinclair H-C Gasoline. $100. *Jackie Knott Collection.*

Sinclair stations of the 1930s displayed this neon clock, promoting Sinclair H-C Gasoline. No listing. *Jackie Knott Collection.*

This advertising poster dates from the early 1930s and advertises Sinclair H-C Gasoline. $35. *Jackie Knott Collection.*

This wartime advertising poster promotes Sinclair dealer services. $35. *Jackie Knott Collection.*

This advertising poster dates from the late 1930s and advertises Sinclair aviation lubricants. $35. *Jackie Knott Collection.*

This advertising poster dates from the early 1930s and advertises Sinclair H-C Gasoline. $35. *Jackie Knott Collection.*

This 1930s advertising poster promotes Sinclair dealer services. $35. *Jackie Knott Collection.*

Sinclair's standard identification sign, used from 1927 until 1958, displayed the famed Sinclair H-C logo. Shown here is a 48" example from the 1930s, but 72" examples are also known to exist, along with curb signs shown in other photos in this book. $350. *Jackie Knott Collection.*

Shown here are station structural signage used in the 1930s. $250-$350. *Jackie Knott Collection.*

This lubester is adorned with a Sinclair "Farm Products" logo. No listing. *Jackie Knott Collection.*

Shown here is an accurate restoration of a Sinclair Opaline lubester from the 1940s. No listing. *Jackie Knott Collection.*

This poster demonstrates motorists' concerns about oil bootlegging. It dates from the early 1930s. $35. *Jackie Knott Collection.*

Sinclair offered their premium motor oils in five quart cans, used for complete oil changes. Shown here is the earliest version of sealed can for Sinclair "Pennsylvania" Motor Oil and a file box for reminder cards used by Sinclair dealers. $125 each. *Jackie Knott Collection.*

Sinclair has used promotional toy trucks through the years, and shown here is a highly desirable fuel oil delivery version from the 1930s. $500. *Jackie Knott Collection.*

Assorted toy trucks from the 1930s, 40s, and 50s, displaying various Sinclair logos. $35-$200.

An assortment of early Sinclair toy trucks. $50-$200. *Jackie Knott Collection.*

Employee lunchrooms at refineries and aboard ocean-going tankers served meals in these Sinclair branded dishes. $25-$100. *Jackie Knott Collection.*

A personalized name badge was part of every Sinclair attendant's uniform. Shown here are two examples from the 1920s and 30s. $75-$100. *Jackie Knott Collection.*

In much of the country Sinclair's motor-grade gasoline was branded simply "US Motor Specifications," a very generic term. Shown here is a three-piece glass globe from the late 1930s. $650-$700. *Scott Benjamin Collection.*

Shown here is a one-piece milk-glass body decaled to advertise Sinclair's motor-grade gasoline, branded simply "US Motor Specifications." Sinclair experimented with decals on blank bodies as they began to phase out one-piece baked-finish globes. They were abandoned shortly thereafter when Sinclair introduced three-piece glass bodies. $1500. *Scott Benjamin Collection.*

Three-piece glass globe from the early 1930s, also advertising the gasoline branded "US Motor Specifications." $700. *Scott Benjamin Collection.*

From 1916 until 1934, Sinclair's regular grade motor fuel was branded simply "Sinclair Gasoline." This three-piece glass globe dates from the 1931-1934 era. $700. *Scott Benjamin Collection.*

Sinclair introduced its premium-grade Sinclair HC Gasoline in 1926. It remained a premium until 1934, when Sinclair Ethyl was introduced, and became Sinclair's regular-grade fuel from 1934 until 1961.

Shown here is an extremely rare one-piece etched Sinclair HC globe, displaying the rare, transitional "striped HC" logo. This logo appeared in 1926 and was replaced by the more familiar red-center logo within six months. No Listing. *Scott Benjamin Collection.*

The first of the familiar three-piece glass Sinclair HC globes is this version with the green areas very dark, almost black in appearance. $400. *Scott Benjamin Collection.*

Perhaps the best known and most desirable of all Sinclair quart motor oil cans are these cans which appeared in 1936 and continued in use until World War II. The standing dinosaur was the predecessor to the "Dino" of the 1960s. $35 each. *Scott Benjamin Collection.*

Sinclair road maps in the 1930s featured elaborate artwork. Shown here is a 1934 map showing a cottage style Sinclair station in the background. $25. *Scott Benjamin Collection.*

The Sinclair brandname appeared on many pieces of railroad rolling stock, and was offered in many model railroad sets. $50. *Scott Benjamin Collection.*

An early Sinclair Super Flame decal is displayed on the storage tank used for dispensing kerosene at a country store in Tennessee.

An extremely rare Parco Ethyl globe, dating from 1928-1930. No listing. *George Kraus Collection.*

Shown here are milk-glass bodies decaled to advertise that product. Sinclair experimented with decals on blank bodies as they began to phase out one-piece baked-finish globes. They were abandoned shortly thereafter when Sinclair introduced three-piece glass bodies. These date from 1932 and are valued at $250-$350 each.

These vintage 1936 lubester signs, complete with majestically standing dinosaur, are among the most popular Sinclair collectibles. *Dan Flaat Collection.* $650-$1000.

Typical Rio Grande station in California in the 1930s. Sinclair motor oils and lubricants are visible through the display windows. *Courtesy Ron Johnson.*

Early Parco one-piece etched globe, unusual in that it displays the local distributor name. No listing. *A. J. Vogel Collection.*

The dealer operating this Sinclair castle station in Crossville, Tennessee, was competing with a Texaco station across the street when this photo was taken in 1946.

Sinclair marketed their heating oils under the brandname "Super Flame." Heating oil is essentially kerosene, and kerosene sold at retail was dispensed from pumps topped with this rare and beautiful globe. $650. *Scott Benjamin Collection.*

This beautiful Sinclair "Castle" station stood on the corner of 16th & The Paseo in Kansas City about 1932. Sinclair continued to build "castle" style stations until the beginning of World War II.

Art-deco Richfield station dating from the mid-1930s. Sinclair (and to a lesser extent Cities Service) investment saved the brand from extinction during the Depression years. *Courtesy Ron Johnson.*

This classic Sinclair station stood on the corner of W. Queen St. and Armistead Ave in Hampton, Virginia. It was photographed here in 1934, and was operating as late as 1968. In 1970, after Sinclair stations in the east had rebranded BP and Hampton had undergone significant urban renewal, a large modern BP station, designed in a unique colonial style, was built on an adjacent site.

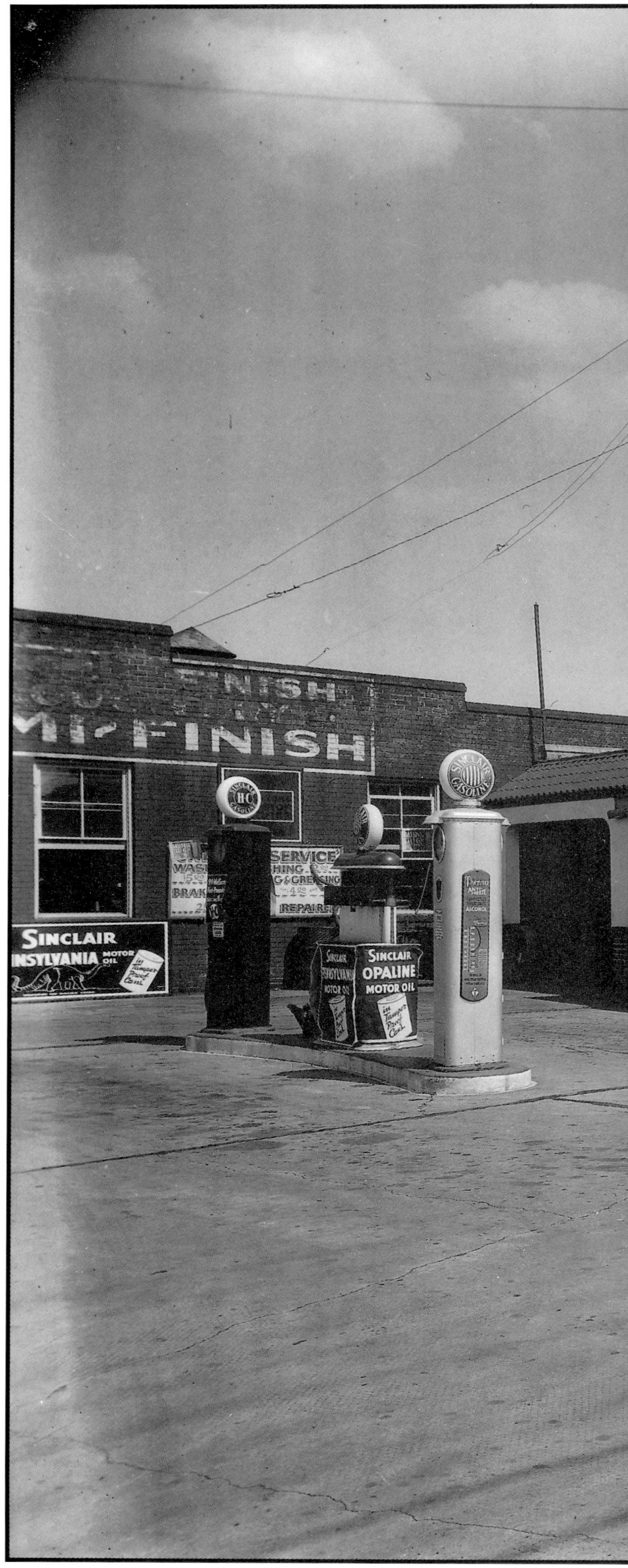

SINCLAIR
SINCLAIR
THE NEW
Firestone
HIGH SPEED TIRE FOR 1934
50%
LONGER
SINCLAIR
OPALINE
MOTOR OIL

Richfield Oil Corporation Of New York

The dual brand Betholine-Sinclair trademark is featured on this 1955 road map. $25. *Wayne Henderson Collection.*

Richfield Oil Corporation of New York was created in August 1929 when the flamboyant and expansion minded Richfield Oil Company of California purchased New York marketers Acewood Petroleum and Walburn Petroleum, merging them to form Richfield Oil Corporation of New York. The company was created with the concept of bringing a well respected brand and source of consistent supply to independent distributors all along the eastern seaboard. When Richfield of California entered receivership in 1931, the expansion of the distributor based was halted for a time. Then, in 1935, Sinclair purchased Richfield of New York and the expansion began again, with a renewed focus on the branding of aggressive jobbers.

Among the most successful relationships was that with Baltimore based Sherwood Brothers. Sherwood was founded prior to 1920 and was marketing a benzol motor fuel under the "Betholine" trademark when the Richfield representative came calling. As a result, stations became dual-brand Betholine-Richfield stations, and were found throughout Maryland, Washington, D.C., and in parts of Virginia and Pennsylvania.

After World War II, Richfield moved to modernize their marketing, encouraging their jobber base to brand the best possible dealers within their territories. The Richfield image easily made the transition to the era of internally illuminated signage, and those signs were displayed at an ever growing number of sites from Maine to Florida.

Gasoline brand names remained Richfield Hi-Octane and Richfield Ethyl throughout much of the company's history, although in 1956 "Premium Richfield" replaced Richfield Ethyl. Motor oils retained the brand names made familiar in the era prior to 1935, and Richfield and Richlube motor oils were available at both Richfield of New York and Richfield of California stations on either coast, different products from different companies sold under the same brand name.

In the end, the elimination of the Richfield brand came quickly. In the summer of 1964 the assets of the Richfield Oil Corporation of New York were totally absorbed into Sinclair Oil Corporation. Overnight, Richfield jobbers became Sinclair jobbers, and stations were reimaged with Sinclair's "Dino" logos and products of that era.

Many oil companies have maintained secondary brands; Conoco with Kayo, Mileage and DS, Ashland with Tri-State, Phillips with Paraland, Pure with Super Par, the Barber brands, and others. The Richfield-Sinclair arrangement was unique, however, in that Richfield was an all jobber company and maintained no direct marketing. Other secondary brands were often salary-operated company direct outlets, or at least company owned and dealer-leased. As an all-jobber operation, Richfield was free to build itself into a network of the best jobbers, and best dealers, within their market. With that in mind, it is no wonder that a struggling Sinclair was eager to incorporate the Richfield marketing into their own. Even after more than thirty years, the Richfield network remains some of BPs most successful marketers, particularly in New England, New York, and Virginia.

Atlantic, Richfield, and Sinclair imaging was in the process of blending to Arco when this 1970 road map was released. $5. *Wayne Henderson Collection.*

In Maryland and in parts of Virginia, Pennsylvania, and Washington, D.C., Sinclair was distributed by a regional marketer known as Sherwood Brothers. Sherwood had, in the years prior to branding first Richfield and later Sinclair, introduced a benzol motor fuel branded "Beth-O-Lene." The Betholene brandname was combined with Richfield in the early 1930s, and in what was the beginning of the end for Richfield of New York, combined with Sinclair in the early postwar years. Stations remained dual-brand Betholene—Sinclair until the late 1950s, when Sinclair purchased Sherwood Brothers outright. Shown here is a dual brand Beth-O-Lene/Sinclair sign from the 1940s. $450-$600. *Jackie Knott Collection.*

Classic die-cut Richfield identification sign, of the design in use when Sinclair purchased Richfield of New York in 1935. $2500. *Ed Natale, Jr. Collection.*

Shortly after Sinclair purchased Richfield of New York, this new logo was introduced. Porcelain signs such as this were displayed at Richfield stations until 1940. $600. *Jim Hollabaugh Collection.*

In 1940 Richfield introduced a much more art-deco image of their eagle and shield. Shown here is a 48" porcelain sign of the type in use from 1940 until the Richfield brand was replaced by Sinclair in 1964. $450.

Richfield globes, showing the product realignment of 1956. $300 each.
Wayne Henderson Collection.

Jarvis Brothers Richfield Station, somewhere in New England, 1932. *Courtesy Thornton Beroth.*

Dominion Oil Company, Richfield distributors in Richmond, Virginia, were operating this station in Richmond in August, 1963. Less than a year later Richfield stations would be rebranded Sinclair and Richfield would pass into history. *Courtesy Walt Wimer, Jr.*

Refinement Of An Image

Sinclair emerged from World War II with its proper name, Sinclair Oil Corporation, reclaimed, and ready for the tasks that lay ahead. In the years immediately following World War II, any marketer could sell every drop of gasoline he could find to sell. Such was the pent-up demand for freedom and mobility that even independents and "off brands," once shunned by all but the most austere motorists, thrived. Sinclair's secondary brand, Richfield (New York), was considered an independent in many markets, and saw amazing growth in the period between 1946 and 1950. Beginning about 1950, however, major oil companies became extremely conscious of their image. Selling a product that the consumer should never see, or come in direct contact with, oil companies had to rely on the image their stations projected to signify whether they offered high quality fuels, or those of lesser quality.

Cardboard toy station promotion, offered by Sinclair in 1953. $100. *Jackie Knott Collection.*

As stated in the previous chapter, Sinclair signs were seen in every state east of the Rocky Mountains. Sinclair's problem here, however, was that those signs couldn't be seen at night. When Shell, in 1947, began experimentation with internally illuminated plexiglass signage, suddenly every other "old fashioned" porcelain sign was outdated. Gasoline marketers scrambled to find suitable illuminated signage, and by 1950 most majors were at least experimenting with plastic signage. Sinclair, in joining this first imaging, had a problem. Their "Sinclair HC Gasoline" sign appeared outdated, was somewhat hard to read or recognize at higher speeds, and with the color combination then in use, could not be made to properly light up when constructed of plastic. With this realization, the search for a new image began.

In the short term, dealers were trained in merchandising their stations, with seminars offered to teach dealers how to make their stations more attractive. Proper lighting was important, and neon overlays were added to existing porcelain signage. New products, beginning with Sinclair Power-X Gasoline, called for the introduction of new images, images which could and would be brighter than those they

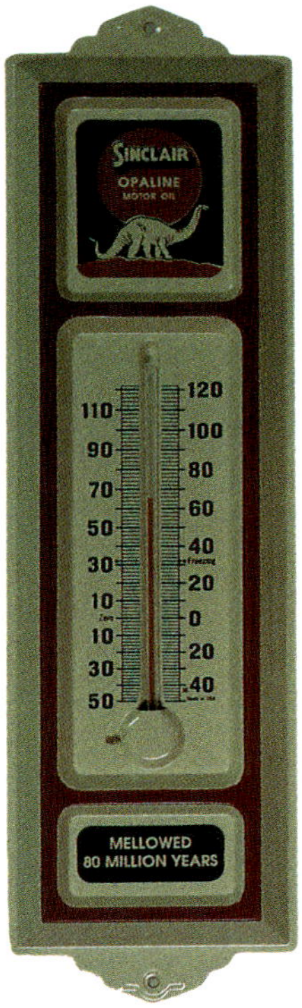

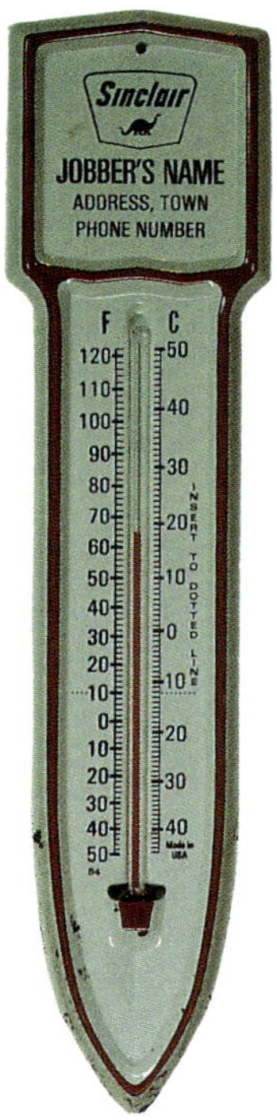

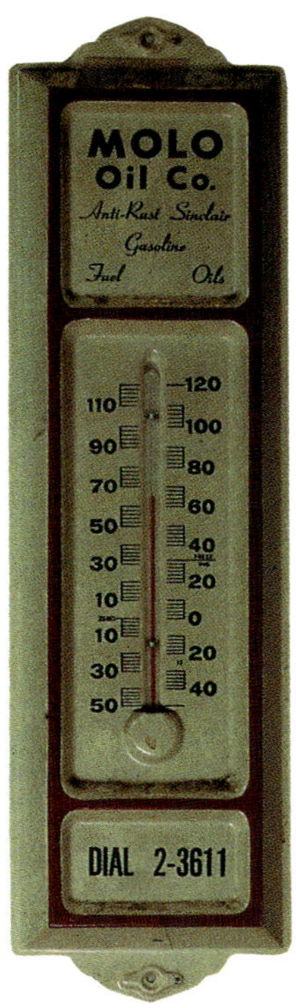

Sinclair advertising thermometers. $25-$100. *Jackie Knott Collection.*

replaced. The cleanliness of stations, always a problem for those marketers who relied heavily on jobbers who, in turn, branded any location available, was emphasized. New station designs were created in gleaming white porcelain, and porcelain panels were installed over existing block, stucco, and brick structures in an effort to improve their presentation to the public.

Oddly enough, Richfield, Sinclair's secondary brand that appeared on jobber supplied stations from Maine to Florida, did not suffer much from the image enhancements of the 1950s. Richfield signage was clean, and the company made the transition well from spot-lit signage to internally illuminated plastic signs.

Numerous image experiments were conducted in the mid-1950s, some of which are detailed in the accompanying sidebar. Despite all the clean-up effort and attempts at improved lighting, the Sinclair image just simply was not modern in a "modern-conscious" 1950s. Sinclair experimented in many markets with the "Triple-Check" image, and certainly had to be nearing the adoption of that image when the "Dino" image was introduced in 1959. For the first time in its history, Sinclair tied their most famous lubricant's image mascot, the brontosaurus, to gasoline marketing. Prior to this time, the brontosaurus, known to all as "Dino," had represented only Sinclair lubricants. The Dino image, initially used in station signage, then in gasoline brand names and images, has proved to be the longest lasting of all major oil company images and continues, albeit on a "controlled background," in use today. Sinclair finally had a sign that could be constructed of plastic, illuminated at night, and project the high-quality clean image they had so long sought. Full implementation of the new signage began in 1959, and by 1962, Dino signs were in place throughout Sinclair's marketing territory.

Along with a new image, new products were introduced in this era, as the postwar horsepower race called for not only improved fuels, but lubricants as well. Sinclair's first high detergent oil, Sinclair Extra Duty, was introduced in 1952, as was Sinclair's first multigrade motor oil, Sinclair Extra Duty Triple X, just over a year later.

Diesel engines in long-haul trucking became much more common in the 1950s, and Sinclair was there with products for this market as well. Sinclair was among the first to introduce a diesel engine oil, Sinclair Tenol, in 1935, and Sinclair began approving a growing list of stations selling diesel fuel as Sinclair Truck Stops or Richfield Truck Stops.

Sinclair marketing expanded in this era through acquisition as well, although not nearly so aggressive as that seen in the 1930s. In 1948 Sinclair purchased the Louisville, Kentucky, based Stoll Refining. Stoll, founded in 1896, was marketed in Indiana and Kentucky under the "Golden Tip" brand name. Golden Tip stations re-branded Sinclair in 1952.

As the 1950s came to a close, Sinclair's sparkling new Dino sign adorned over 29,000 stations in thirty-eight states. Richfield's cream and blue Soaring Eagle appeared on over 3,500 stations in fourteen states, including some New England territory that Sinclair did not market in. In the mid-Atlantic area Sherwood Brothers, a large jobber operating under the Betholine-Richfield and Betholine-Sinclair brand names added hundreds more to the total. It would be the high point of Sinclair's marketing extent.

During the 1950s Sinclair stations that accepted the proprietary Sinclair credit card displayed this sign for the convenience of passing motorists. $125. *Jackie Knott Collection.*

This hanging mobile displays numerous Sinclair products offered about 1955. $400-$500. *Jackie Knott Collection.*

A Sinclair ocean-going tanker is shown in the photographic print from the 1950s. $250. *Jackie Knott Collection.*

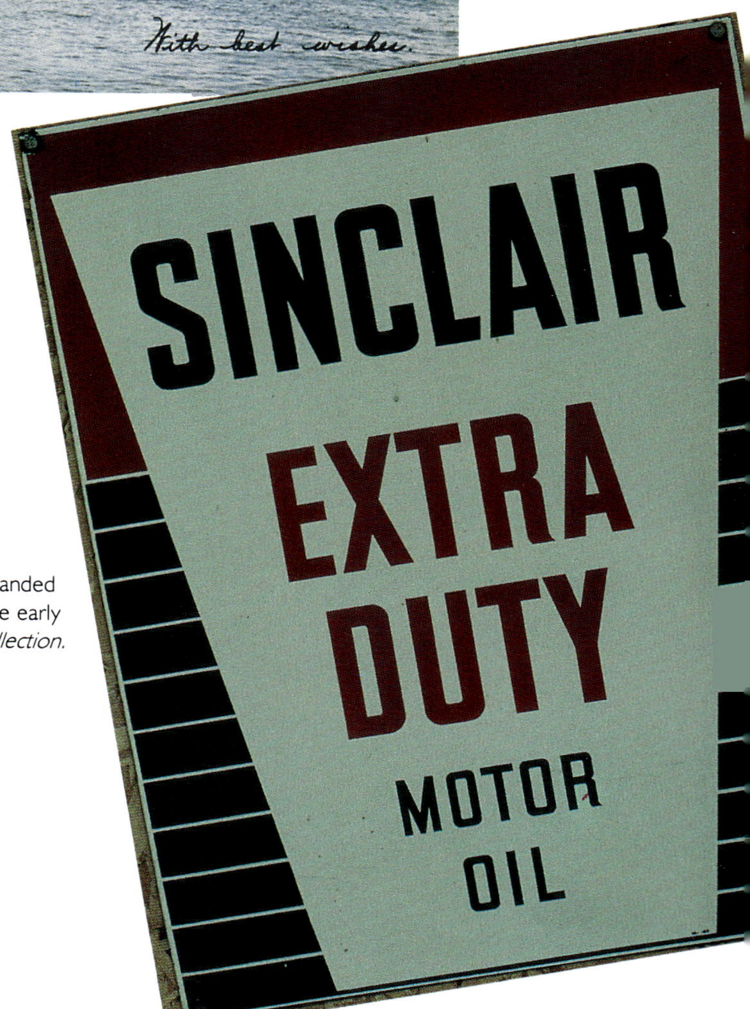

In 1952 Sinclair introduced their first modern-era, detergent motor oil branded "Sinclair Extra Duty." This porcelain hanging sign reproduces the design of the early can and dates from 1952-1955. $150-$250. *Jackie Knott Collection.*

Commonly used as secondary signage at bulk plants, the postwar porcelain "No Smoking" signs are available in either red or green lettering. $40-$50.
Jackie Knott Collection.

Prior to 1958, when the "Dino" logo was introduced, Sinclair Oil and Gas, Sinclair's exploration division, used a logo basically unchanged from that in use since 1916. This porcelain sign is available in both 6" ($600-$800) and 12" ($300-$600), and despite its appearance as an item from the 1920s, is more likely to date from the 1950s. *Jackie Knott Collection.*

This die-cut cardboard sign from the early 1950s advertises Sinclair automotive services. $350-$400. *Jackie Knott Collection.*

Sinclair stations, bulk plants, and other properties were painted in appropriate Sinclair colors with paint supplied by the company. Shown here are various Sinclair paint cans. $15-$25.
Jackie Knott Collection.

Assorted steel one-quart motor oil cans used during the 1950s. $20-$75.
Jackie Knott Collection.

Assorted steel five-quart cans used during the 1930s, 40s, and 50s. Primarily premium grade motor oils were offered in five quart packages for complete oil-change sales. $35-$150.
Jackie Knott Collection.

Assorted Sinclair Anti-Freeze cans from the 1930s through the 1960s. $25-$100.
Jackie Knott Collection.

In 1956, when the octane rating of Sinclair Power-X gasoline was improved, this globe hood was attached to gas pump globes to call attention to the new product. $300. *Jackie Knott Collection.*

These wooden miniatures were used by Sinclair area representatives to show dealers examples of signage available to them for co-operative advertising opportunities. No listing. *Jackie Knott Collection.*

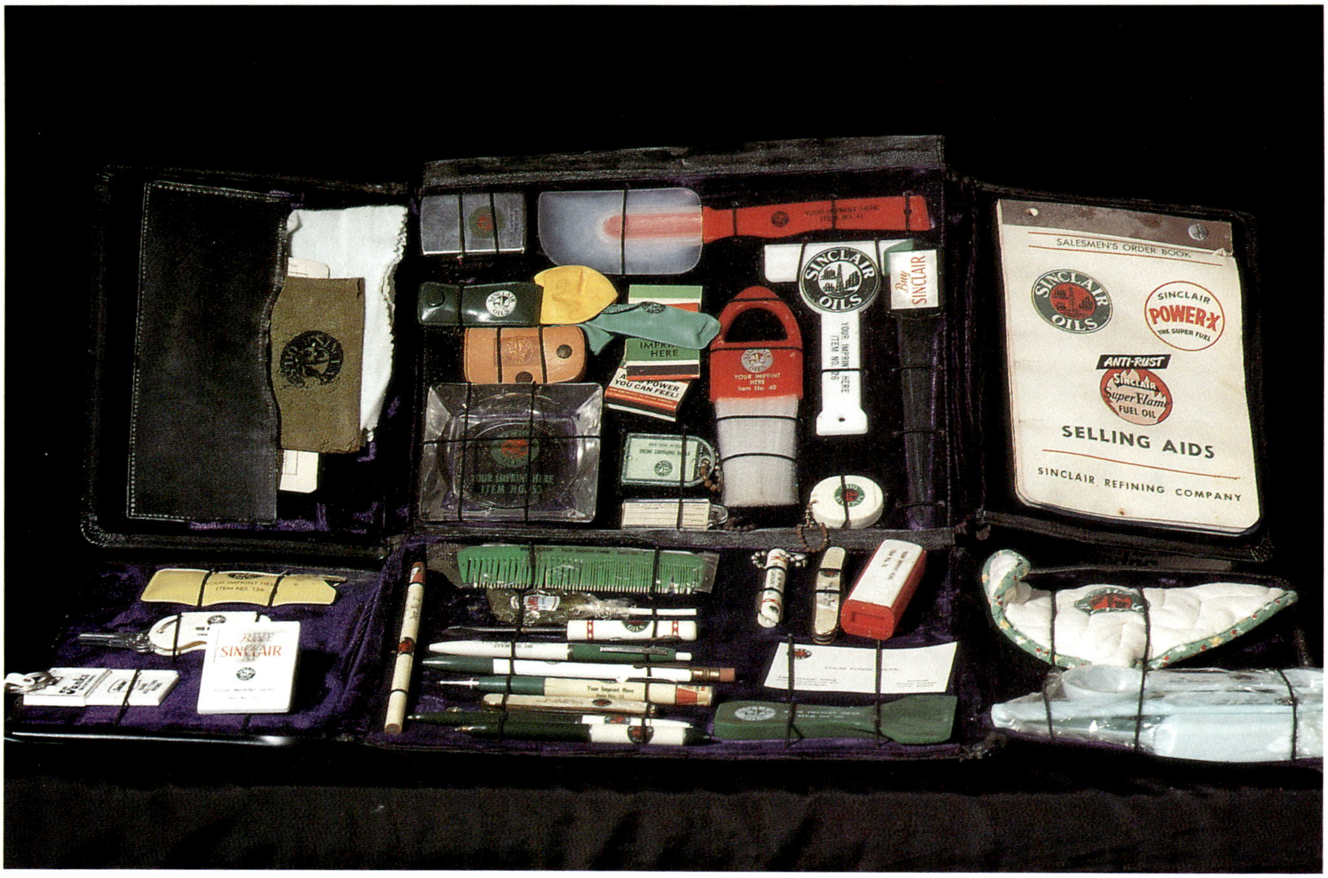

Sinclair area representatives carried these sample cases to show dealers examples of advertising novelties available to them. $450. *Jackie Knott Collection.*

These flags were left with service station employees to indicate to a dealer who was away that a Sinclair area representative had called on them in their absence. $50. *Jackie Knott Collection.*

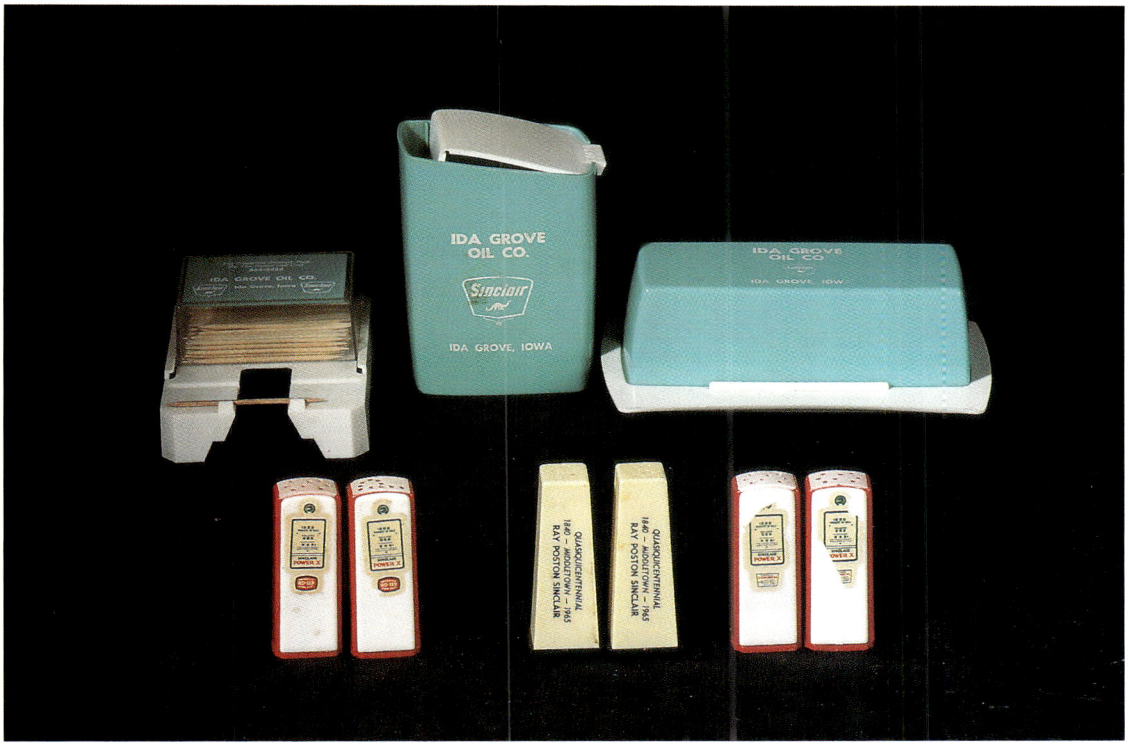

Assorted tableware items were available for local station promotion. Dealer name and location could be imprinted on them for seasonal give-aways. $25-$100. *Jackie Knott Collection.*

This cardboard hat was part of a toy promotion offered by Sinclair in the 1950s. $100. *Jackie Knott Collection.*

A Sinclair ocean-going tanker is shown in this photo print. $250.
Jackie Knott Collection.

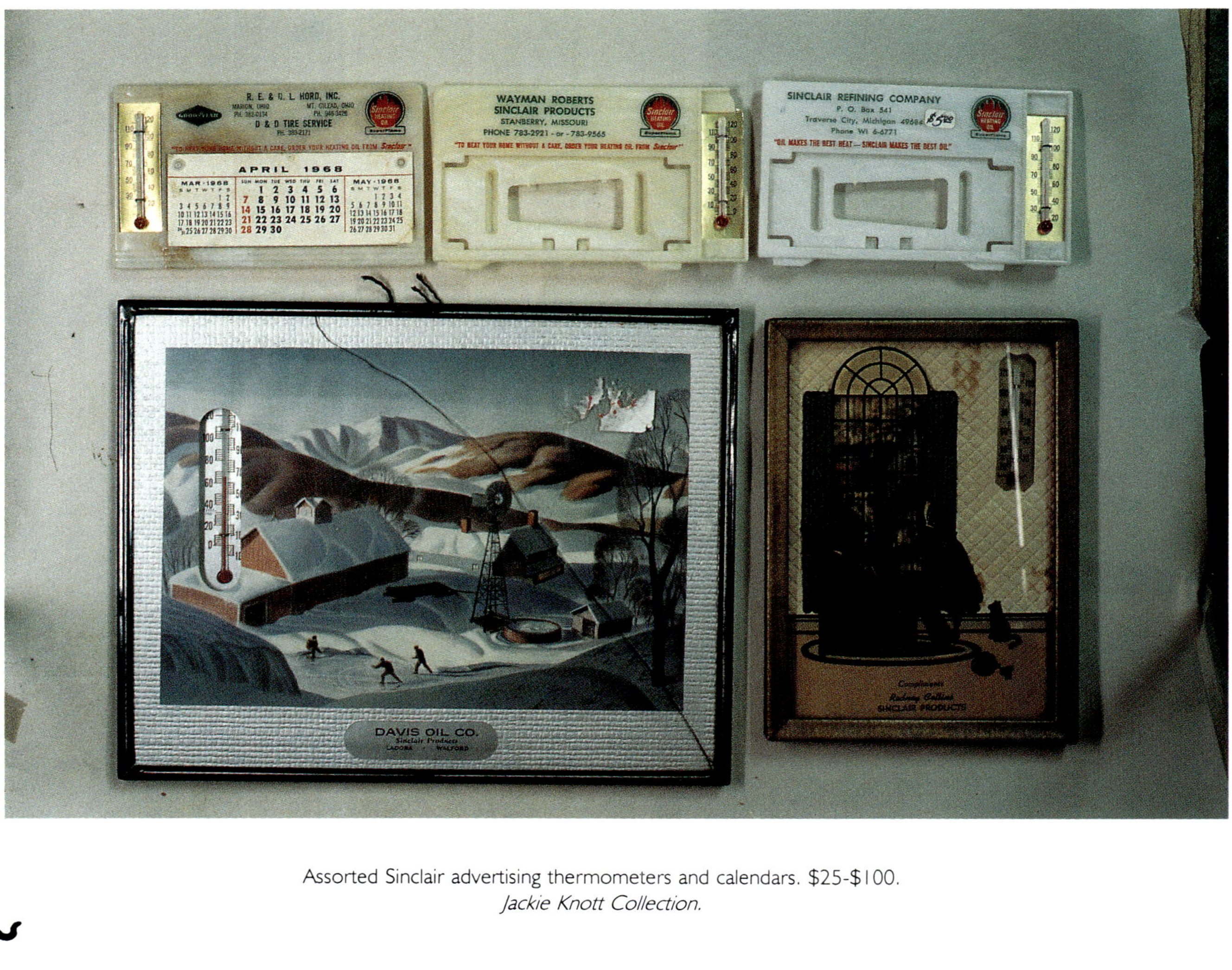

Assorted Sinclair advertising thermometers and calendars. $25-$100.
Jackie Knott Collection.

Shown here are assorted Sinclair dealer promotional items. $25-$100. *Jackie Knott Collection.*

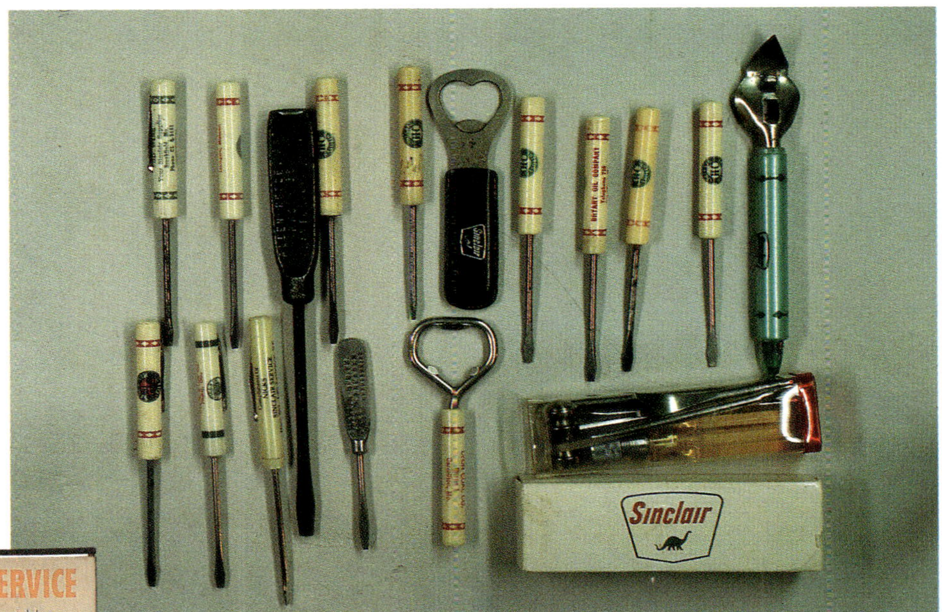

Assorted Sinclair screwdrivers and other promotional hardware. $25-$100. *Jackie Knott Collection.*

Shown here is an assortment of road maps from the 1940s, displayed in a 1950s road map rack. $100. *Jackie Knott Collection.*

These signs offer various guarantees of Sinclair Rest Room cleanliness. $25-$100. *Jackie Knott Collection.*

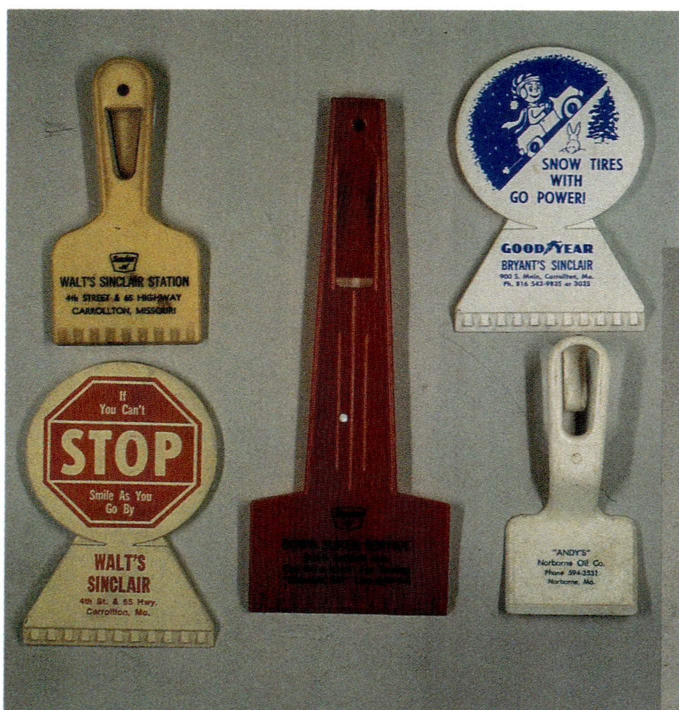

Another popular promotional item for Sinclair marketers were ice scrapers. Shown here are various examples. $25-$50. *Jackie Knott Collection.*

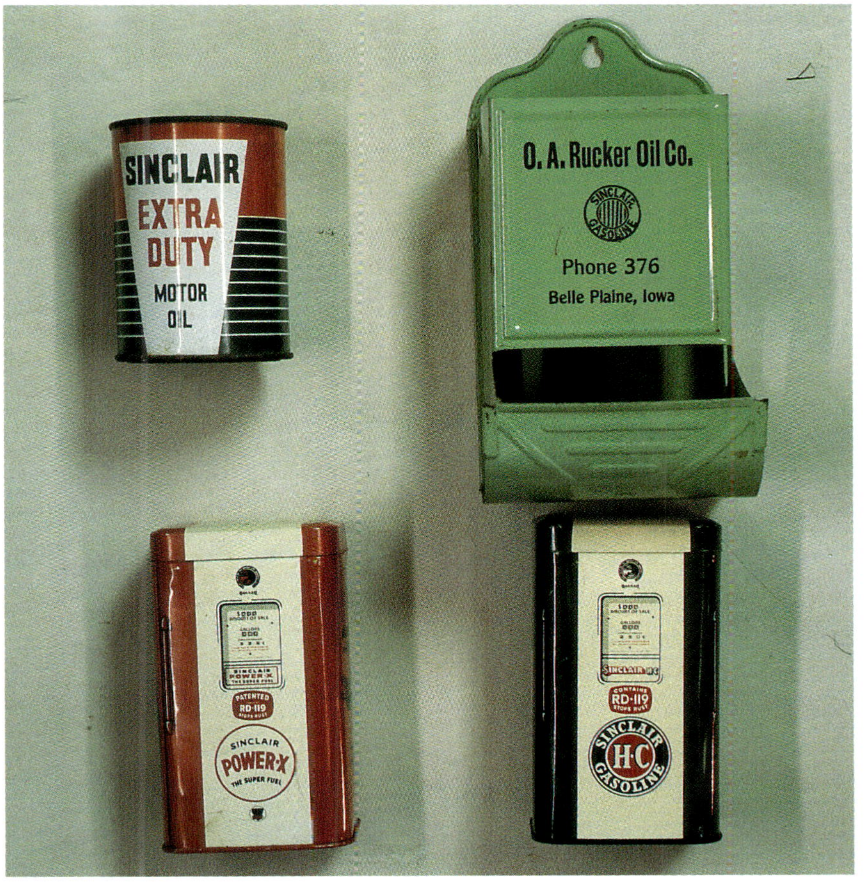

Tin-litho promotional items, including coin banks and a k tchen-match holder. $25-$100. *Jackie Knott Collection.*

Very popular items among collectors, this photo shows an assortment of Sinclair household oil and lighter fluid cans. $25-$50. *Jackie Knott Collection.*

Among the most popular promotional items of the postwar era were ashtrays. Shown here are numerous examples. $25-$50. *Jackie Knott Collection.*

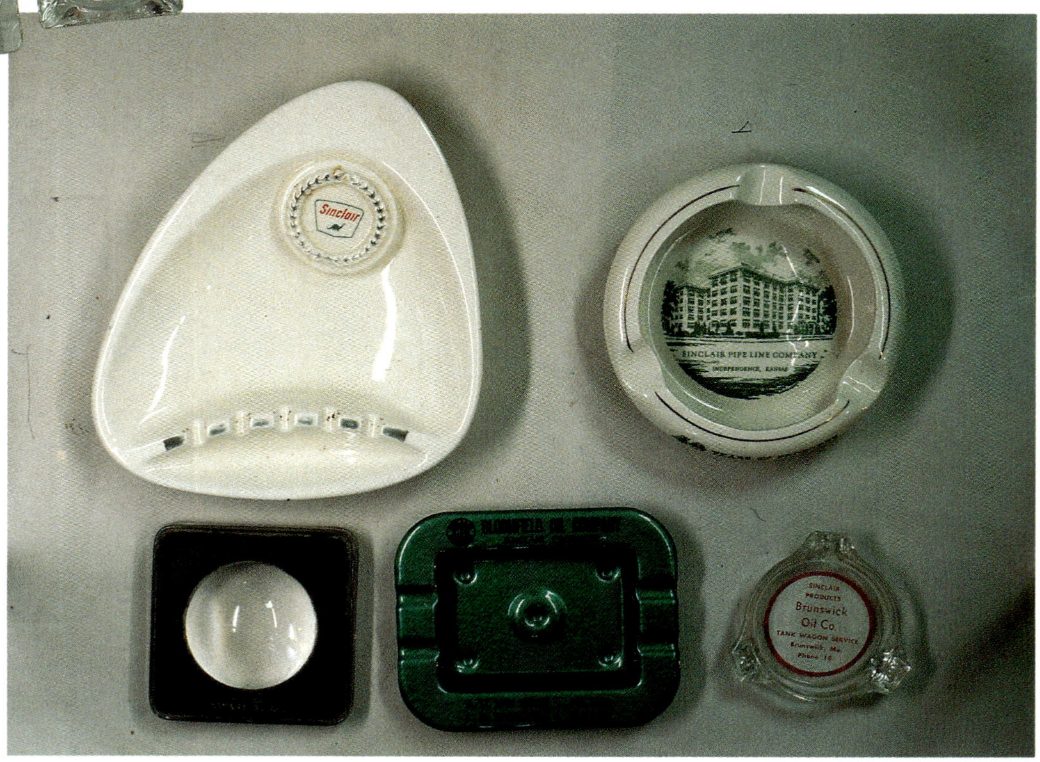

An extremely rare credit card acceptance chart from the 1940s. $100. *Jackie Knott Collection.*

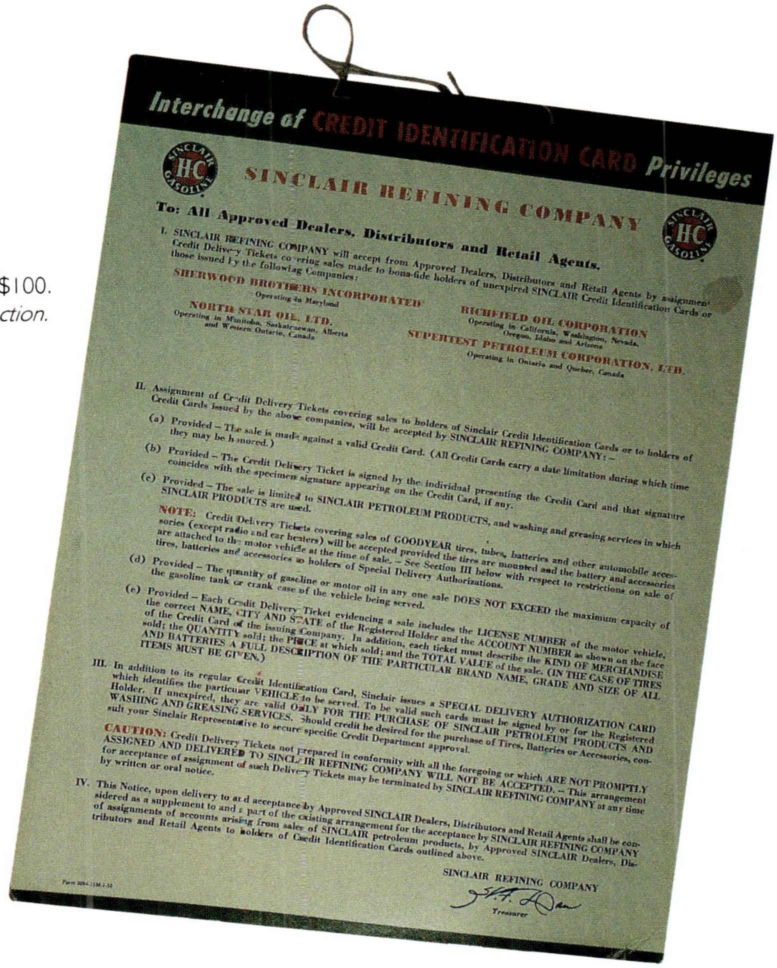

Interchange of CREDIT IDENTIFICATION CARD Privileges

SINCLAIR REFINING COMPANY

To: All Approved Dealers, Distributors and Retail Agents.

I. SINCLAIR REFINING COMPANY will accept from Approved Dealers, Distributors and Retail Agents by assignment Credit Delivery Tickets covering sales made to bona-fide holders of unexpired SINCLAIR Credit Identification Cards or those issued by the following Companies:

SHERWOOD BROTHERS INCORPORATED
Operating in Maryland

NORTH STAR OIL, LTD.
Operating in Manitoba, Saskatchewan, Alberta and Western Ontario, Canada

RICHFIELD OIL CORPORATION
Operating in California, Washington, Nevada, Oregon, Idaho and Arizona

SUPERTEST PETROLEUM CORPORATION, LTD.
Operating in Ontario and Quebec, Canada

II. Assignment of Credit Delivery Tickets covering sales to holders of Sinclair Credit Identification Cards or to holders of Credit Cards issued by the above companies, will be accepted by SINCLAIR REFINING COMPANY: –

(a) Provided – The sale is made against a valid Credit Card. (All Credit Cards carry a date limitation during which time they may be honored.)

(b) Provided – The Credit Delivery Ticket is signed by the individual presenting the Credit Card and that signature coincides with the specimen signature appearing on the Credit Card, if any.

(c) Provided – The sale is limited to SINCLAIR PETROLEUM PRODUCTS, and washing and greasing services in which SINCLAIR PRODUCTS are used.

NOTE: Credit Delivery Tickets covering sales of GOODYEAR tires, tubes, batteries and other automobile accessories (except radio and car heaters) will be accepted provided the tires are mounted and the battery and accessories are attached to the motor vehicle at the time of sale. – See Section III below with respect to restrictions on sale of tires, batteries and accessories to holders of Special Delivery Authorizations.

(d) Provided – The quantity of gasoline or motor oil in any one sale DOES NOT EXCEED the maximum capacity of the gasoline tank or crank case of the vehicle being served.

(e) Provided – Each Credit Delivery Ticket evidencing a sale includes the LICENSE NUMBER of the motor vehicle, the correct NAME, CITY AND STATE of the Registered Holder and the ACCOUNT NUMBER as shown on the face of the Credit Card of the issuing Company. In addition, each ticket must describe the KIND OF MERCHANDISE sold; the QUANTITY sold; the PRICE at which sold; and the TOTAL VALUE of the sale. (IN THE CASE OF TIRES AND BATTERIES A FULL DESCRIPTION OF THE PARTICULAR BRAND NAME, GRADE AND SIZE OF ALL ITEMS MUST BE GIVEN.)

III. In addition to its regular Credit Identification Card, Sinclair issues a SPECIAL DELIVERY AUTHORIZATION CARD which identifies the particular VEHICLE to be served. To be valid such cards must be signed by or for the Registered Holder. If unexpired, they are valid ONLY FOR THE PURCHASE OF SINCLAIR PETROLEUM PRODUCTS AND WASHING AND GREASING SERVICES. Should credit be desired for the purchase of Tires, Batteries or Accessories, consult your Sinclair Representative to secure specific Credit Department approval.

CAUTION: Credit Delivery Tickets not prepared in conformity with all the foregoing or which ARE NOT PROMPTLY ASSIGNED AND DELIVERED TO SINCLAIR REFINING COMPANY WILL NOT BE ACCEPTED. – This arrangement for acceptance of assignment of such Delivery Tickets may be terminated by SINCLAIR REFINING COMPANY at any time by written or oral notice.

IV. This Notice, upon delivery to and acceptance by Approved SINCLAIR Dealers, Distributors and Retail Agents shall be considered as a supplement to and a part of the existing arrangement for the acceptance by SINCLAIR REFINING COMPANY of assignments of accounts arising from sales of SINCLAIR petroleum products, by Approved SINCLAIR Dealers, Distributors and Retail Agents to holders of Credit Identification Cards outlined above.

SINCLAIR REFINING COMPANY

Treasurer

Sinclair ad glasses from the 1940s and 50s, including the highly desirable "dinosaur" glass, used as side glass in Bennett 541 pumps and others with four glass panels. $25-$100. *Jackie Knott Collection.*

Assorted Sinclair ad glass from the 1940s and 50s. $25-$100. *Jackie Knott Collection.*

Writing instruments of all kinds have always been popular promotional pieces. Shown here are numerous examples labeled for Sinclair jobbers and dealers. $25-$100. *Jackie Knott Collection.*

Sinclair promotional knives, often offered as sales incentives. $25-$100. *Jackie Knott Collection.*

Cigarette lighters were used as sales incentives for lubricants salesman, as well as safety awards and other promotions. Shown here are an assortment of Sinclair branded cigarette lighters. $25-$100. *Jackie Knott Collection.*

Sinclair promotional items, corporate and jobber branded. $25-$100. *Jackie Knott Collection.*

Sinclair desk sets and other promotional items. $25-$100. *Jackie Knott Collection.*

Assorted Sinclair promotional items. $25-$100. *Jackie Knott Collection.*

Calendars are an ever-popular oil company promotion, and Sinclair marketers usec these examples, among others, to promote Sinclair products. $25-$100. *Jackie Knott Collection.*

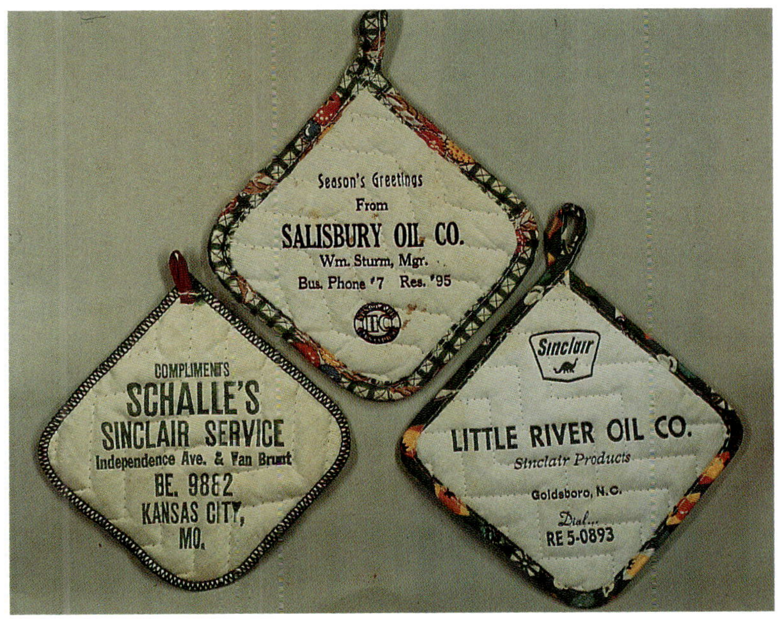

Even potholders were imprinted with Sinclair logos and promotions. $15. *Jackie Knott Collection.*

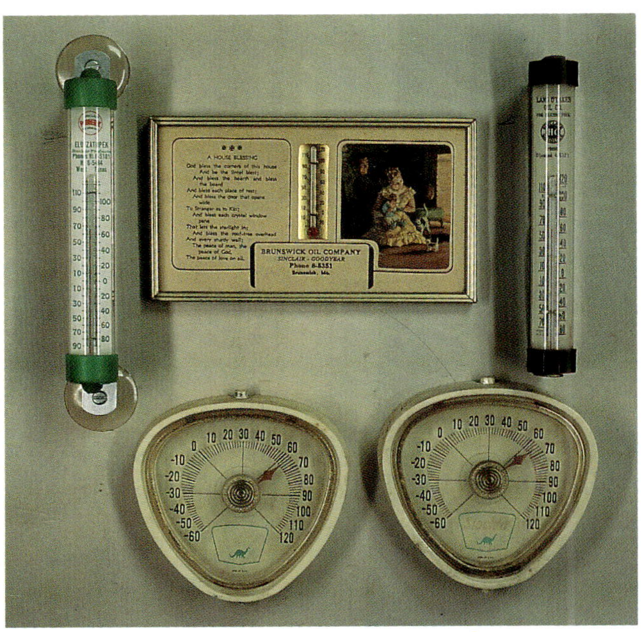

Assor:ed thermometers, all bearing the Sinclair trademarks. $25-$100. *Jackie Knott Collection.*

Gas pumps manufactured by National were adorned with art-deco styling and curved ad glass panels. This Sinclair Power-X ad glass dates from 1953 and is curved to fit National Model A-38 pumps. Curved glass for Sinclair HC and Ethyl are also known.
$250 pair. *Jackie Knott Collection.*

Sinclair offered numerous products for marine and outboard engine usage. In addition to fuels, these lubricants were available. $25-$100.
Jackie Knott Collection.

Wall calendars are ever popular promotional items, and Sinclair jobbers and dealers nationwide offered examples of the assortment shown here. $25-$100. *Jackie Knott Collection.*

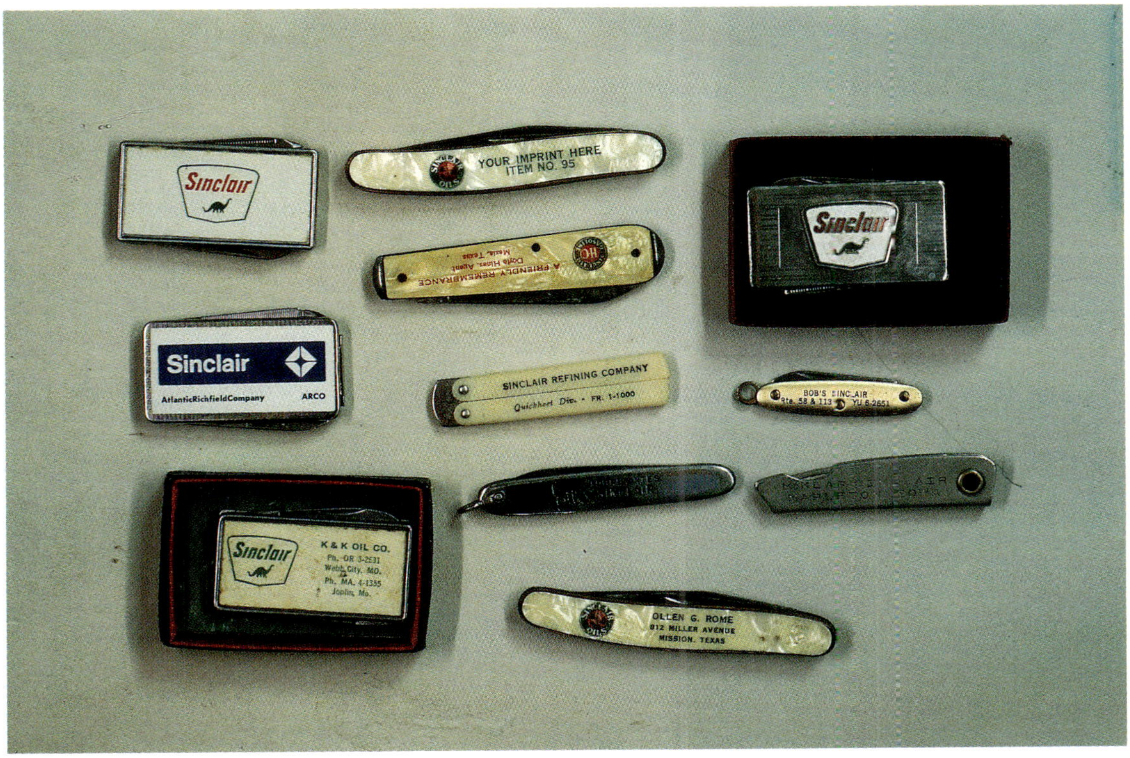

Assorted pocketknives displaying the Sinclair logo. $25-$100. *Jackie Knott Collection.*

Matches were a very economical promotional give-away, and numerous designs of matchbooks advertising Sinclair products are available. $5-$10. *Jackie Knott Collection.*

Sinclair offered several children's shirts advertising Sinclair products. Shown here is one from about 1954. $25. *Jackie Knott Collection.*

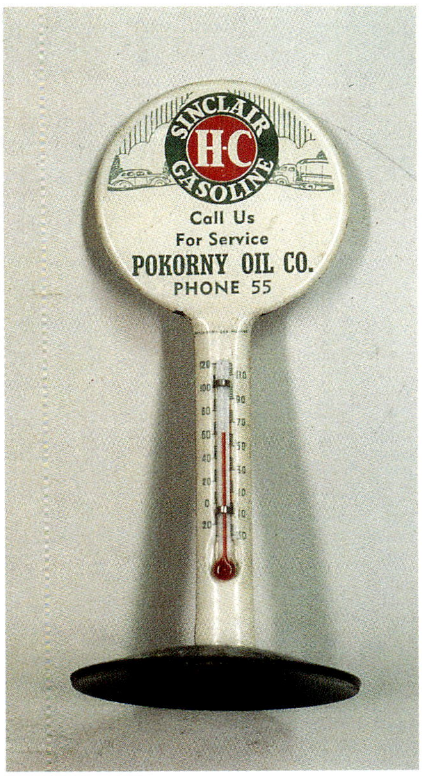

Shown here is an unusual Sinclair tin-litho thermometer. No listing. *Jackie Knott Collection.*

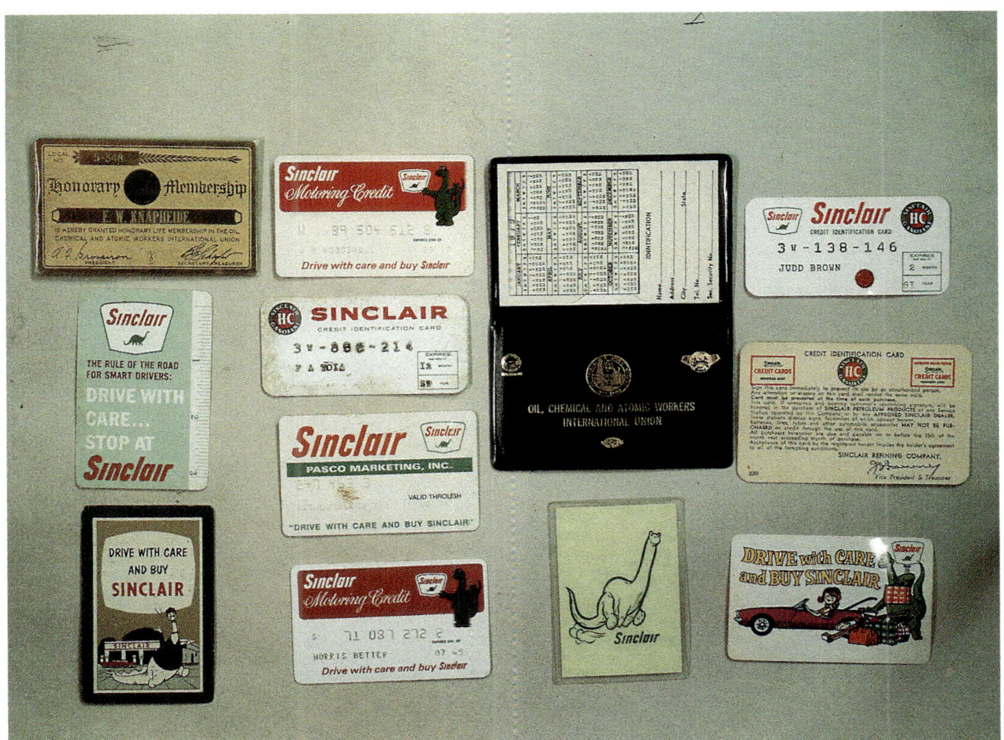

Among the rarest of all branded gasoline collectibles are credit cards. Shown here are numerous Sinclair cards over the years. $25-$100. *Jackie Knott Collection.*

Shown here are coasters displaying the Sinclair logo. $15. *Jackie Knott Collection.*

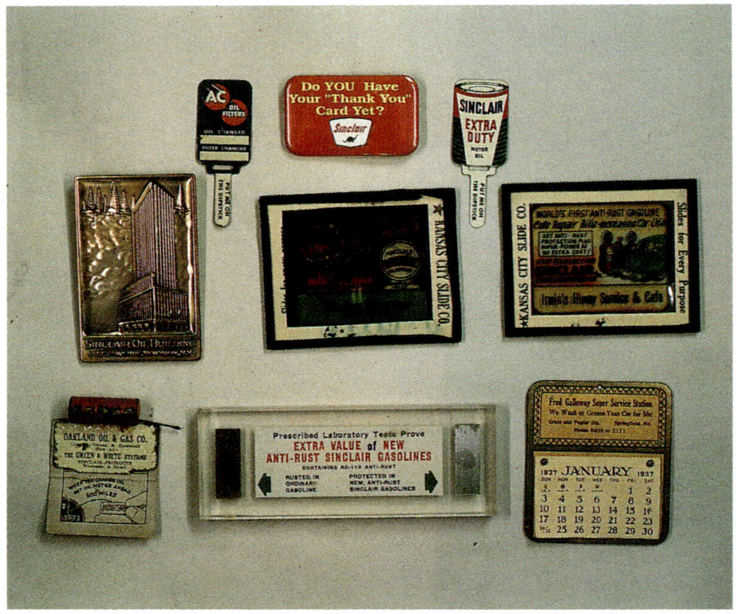

Assorted Sinclair promotional items. $25-$100. *Jackie Knott Collection.*

An enterprising Sinclair distributor in Iowa supplied his dealers with this handy receipt box, complete with reorder reminder tabs. $35. *Jackie Knott Collection.*

Shown here is a Sinclair Power-X outdoor thermometer from 1953. $200. *Jackie Knott Collection.*

Shown here is a Sinclair H-C outdoor thermometer from the late 1940s. $100 *Jackie Knott Collection.*

As the Sinclair logo has evolved, uniform patches have kept up with the design. Shown here are numerous patches displaying logos used throughout this century. $10-$50. *Jackie Knott Collection.*

These postwar advertising posters promote Sinclair dealer services. $35. *Jackie Knott Collection.*

This extremely rare poster dates from the 1950s and advertises Sinclair's sponsorship of comedian Red Skelton's television program. $50. *Jackie Knott Collection.*

This 1956 poster is part of an advertising campaign developed around an increase in Sinclair Power-X octane rating. $35. *Jackie Knott Collection.*

Sinclair has used promotional toy trucks through the years, and shown here is a highly desirable tin litho version from 1953. $450.
Jackie Knott Collection.

Later versions of the three-piece glass Sinclair HC globes are painted a much lighter green. $400. *Scott Benjamin Collection.*

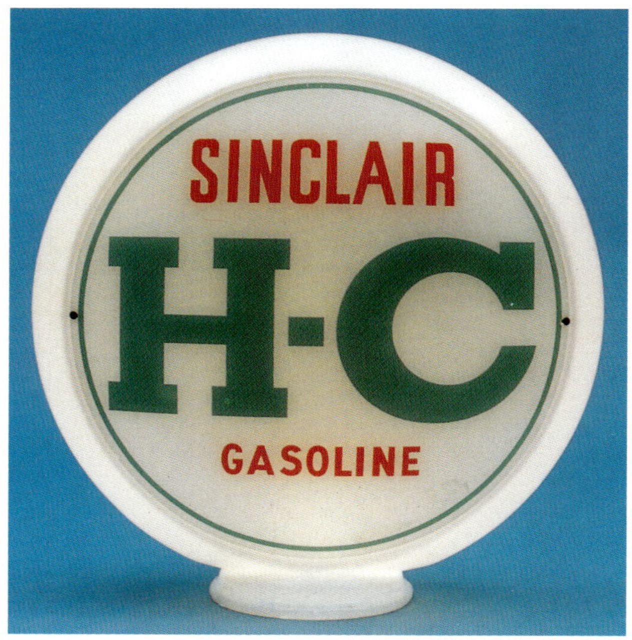

Following a brief experiment with branding Sinclair HC as a "high test," this revised Sinclair HC image was introduced in 1953. $350 on glass, $250 on plastic. *Scott Benjamin Collection.*

An extremely rare Sinclair HC error globe. The green is actually 180 degrees out of register (look at the photo upside down), and appears to be imprinted backwards. It stands testament to the relative availability of Sinclair globes that an error globe like this even exists. This single lens is the only error of its kind known in our hobby. No Listing. *Scott Benjamin Collection.*

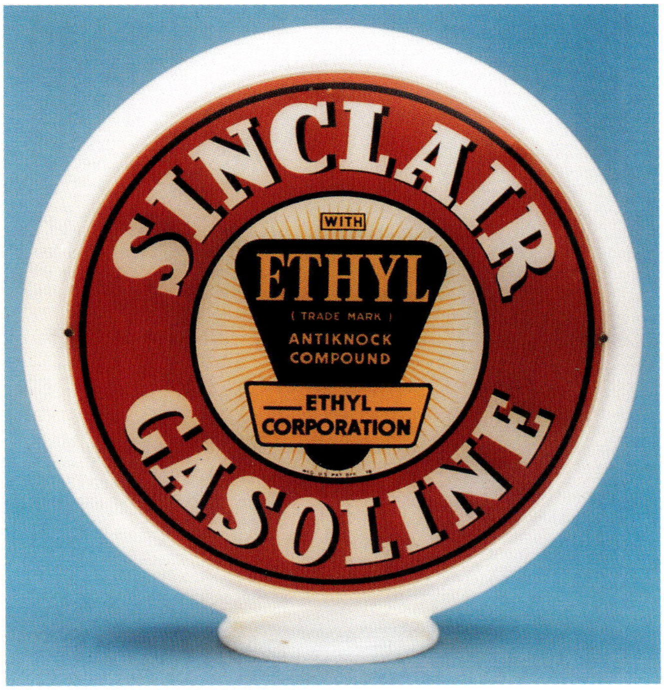

The Sinclair Ethyl globe was redesigned in 1947. This globe design also incorporates the newer "Ethyl Corporation" banner. $750. *Scott Benjamin Collection.*

In 1953 Sinclair Power-X was introduced as Sinclair's premium gasoline. As part of an advertising campaign, this Power-X globe, covered with a decal displaying only a question mark, was used in the introduction of the new product. Most decals were simply peeled off to reveal the normal lens, but a few of these temporarily decaled globes survived. $450. *Scott Benjamin Collection.*

In 1956 an advertising campaign for Sinclair Power-X indicated that the premium product was now rated at over 100 octane. New globes attesting to that fact were introduced for that promotion. $350 on glass, $250 on plastic. *Scott Benjamin Collection.*

The Sinclair Power-X globe, as it appeared after its 1953 introduction. Vivid color makes this rather plain globe into one of the better Sinclair globes. $350. *Scott Benjamin Collection.*

In 1959 the Sinclair "Dino" logo was added to the Power-X globe. Power-X remained Sinclair's premium grade until 1962, when Sinclair Dino Supreme was introduced. $350 on glass, $250 on plastic. *Scott Benjamin Collection.*

Sinclair products were advertised by numerous interesting and decorative ad glass panels through the years. Shown here are ad glasses from the 1930s, 40s, and 50s. $15-$50 *Scott Benjamin Collection.*

Reinstalled by a collector of petroleum memorabilia, this 6' porcelain Sinclair H-C sign of postwar vintage is displayed against a background of the North Carolina mountains, near Dillard, Georgia.

A typical collector assortment of cans, including most of the more commonly available cans from the 1930s, 40s, and 50s. *Aaron Hop Collection.* $10-$50.

Throughout much of its history, Sinclair specified the use of Bennett gas pumps wherever possible. The pre-war Bennett 541 is often thought of as the "classic" Sinclair pump. Shown here is a Bennett 541 restored to Sinclair specifications and accurate except for the pump sign (it dates from 1961). *Carroll Lawson Collection.* $2000-$2500.

The final incarnation of the Sinclair HC logo is this 6' version in shining porcelain. *Eric Bair Collection.* $250.

Opposite page photos:

Top: Chapman Highway in Knoxville, Tennessee, was in a period of "development" in the early 1950s when this Sinclair station was built. *Chip Flohe Collection.*

Bottom: In the postwar years every major oil company developed porcelain-box style stations. This Memphis location was typical of Sinclair's 1950s porcelain station design and is visually a near perfect image of the design. *Chip Flohe Collection.*

SINCLAIR

SINCLAIR
HC
GASOLINE
INCLAIR
SINCLAIR

SINCLAIR
SINCLAIR
S
PEPSI COLA BOTTLING CO.
HC

SINCLAIR
SINCLAIR
SINCLAIR

Opposite page photos:
Top: Sinclair also experimented with attached canopies in the early postwar years. Primarily used in locations in the south, this station stands along Magnolia Avenue in Knoxville, Tenesse. *Chip Flohe Collection.*

Bottom: Rooftop neon signage announces this Knoxville Sinclair station in 1954. *Chip Flohe Collection.*

Sinclair was one of the earliest oil companies to market products specifically for diesel engines, having introduced Tenol Motor Oil, a specialty diesel oil, in 1935. This three-piece glass globe advertises Sinclair's Diesel Fuel and dates from the early postwar era. $400. *Scott Benjamin Collection.*

Sinclair also offered special Marine fuels, as is advertised by this early 1950s Sinclair Marine Gasoline globe. $450. *Scott Benjamin Collection.*

Before and after views of the same station, adorned with Sinclair's latest image package from the mid 1950s.

This beautiful porcelain Sinclair station was standing on the corner of Plymouth Road and Longacre Avenue in Dearborn, Michigan, in 1955. Shown here are day and night shots taken before Sinclair's latest image package was applied.

Here and on the following page we see the same station shown as above, now complete with Sinclair's imaging. Every feature stands out, and color is carefully co-ordinated to attract the passing motorists.

Another view of the station on the previous page.

Experimental Images

Of all the oil company experimental imaging programs ever used, today we are probably most familiar with those used by Sinclair. In the 1920s Sinclair's first temporary or "experimental" image included the addition of the letters "HC" to a circle superimposed over the center stripes on Sinclair signage and globes then in use. This approach was probably chosen to maintain continuity of the image then in use. The "striped HC" logo was used less than a year, when the familiar Sinclair HC Gasoline logo complete with red center circle was introduced.

Another experiment about which we can only guess is the use of the wording "High Compression" on an otherwise normal Sinclair globe. The one known example, found in a city bordering Canada, is thought to have been designed to compete with Supertest "High Compression" gasoline, offered just on the other side of the border.

In Sinclair's search for a brighter image in 1953, Sinclair HC Gasoline was offered as Sinclair Hi-Test HC in several markets. Sinclair Power-X Gasoline, introduced as a premium fuel replacing Sinclair Ethyl, was the first Sinclair brand-image in many years to be identified by a globe that was primarily white, in keeping with the desire to brighten stations. One experiment from this era from which collectibles are known was the covering of the Sinclair Power-X globe lens with a large silver decal with a question mark. No doubt this was connected to a promotional campaign used in the introduction of the product. In conjunction with the introduction of Power-

Sinclair's regular grade "H-C Gasoline" globe, displaying the experimental "triple check" design. $750. *Scott Benjamin Collection.*

X, Sinclair HC pumps were reimaged with primarily white Sinclair Hi-Test HC globes. This experiment was short-lived, since the designation "Hi-Test" for a regular grade product was confusing to motorists and illegal in some states. A redesigned Sinclair HC Gasoline globe, primarily white, was the accepted replacement for the earlier "red circle" HC.

Sinclair's best known "experimental" image was the 1956 introduction of the "Triple Check" logo. The new station signage and pump imaging was installed and introduced in selected cities nationwide, including Macon, Georgia; Morristown, Tennessee; Greenwich, Connecticut; Fort Wayne, Indiana; and Salt Lake City, Utah. It featured a white background, large red Sinclair lettering, and a blue field at the top adorned by the abstract check-marks in red, white, and green. Signs were manufactured in a traditional round and a new trapezoidal shape, a modification of which was eventually used to create the "dino" logo. Pump globes, Sinclair HC and Sinclair Power-X, are found with the triple-check logo as well. This marketing experiment continued at various locations through 1959, when the "Dino" logo replaced Sinclair HC and all experimental images. The "Dino" logo remains in use today.

The sheer magnitude of Sinclair's marketing presence in the 1950s can be seen in the surviving experimental logo items. Most oil company image experiments are low-key, and few see any surviving collectibles. Sinclair was large enough that even though I'm sure some effort was made to keep these "experimental" image items out of the hands of anyone outside the company, a surprising number of these items survive today, prized by fortunate collectors of petroleum memorabilia.

In 1953 Sinclair began experimentation with new logo designs to replace the dated H-C sign. Several designs saw experimentation, but the best known experimental logo is seen here in one of two known sign formats. Commonly referred to as the "triple-check" design, this logo appears on globes and station signage and was used on an experimental basis in various towns around the country including Macon, Georgia; Morristown, Tennessee; Fort Wayne, Indiana; and Salt Lake City, Utah. $750. *Jackie Knott Collection.*

This Sinclair "Hi-Test" HC globe was an example of logo experimentation that began in 1953. Notice the similarity in format to the Sinclair Power-X globe introduced that year. No Listing. *Jackie Knott Collection.*

Taken from the pages of the March 1959 *Service Station Management*, the photos from this article on Sinclair service station design display the usage of the triple-check logo well.

Designed for use where the small 48" H-C signs had been displayed, this 48" Sinclair "Triple-Check" sign is an extremely rare find. $500-$700 *Jackie Knott Collection.*

Competing with Supertest "HC High Compression" in some US cities along the Canadian border (Supertest being a Canadian marketer), Sinclair briefly experimented with this special HC "High Compression" globe in the late 1920s. This one-piece baked-finish globe is dated 1929. No Listing. *Scott Benjamin Collection.*

The experimental "triple check" logo graces this 1956 Sinclair Power-X globe. $750. *Scott Benjamin Collection.*

Macon, Georgia was one of the towns selected for experimentation with Sinclair's "Triple Check" image in 1956. This station was photographed in the spring of 1962, and the triple check signage would soon be replaced with the "Dino" image, introduced in 1958-59.

Dino Era & Lean Years

Image problems conquered, Sinclair entered the 1960s at its strongest point ever. Moving forward to build stations along the nation's ever increasing network of interstate highways and in the suburbs while holding onto their traditional inner-city and rural markets, Sinclair met headlong with reality.

Image enhancement is expensive, and maintaining a far flung network of stations is impractical if you cannot adequately supply those stations with products that can be sold at a profit. Severe crude oil shortages engulfed virtually every mid-size major oil company in the early 1960s, and Sinclair's refineries operated far below their capacity. Crude oil purchases resembled stock market trading as oil companies found themselves in bidding wars among each other for crude produced by a growing number of independent exploration and production companies. Meanwhile, marketing executives established jobber contracts and opened stations, seemingly oblivious to the need to keep refineries and a distribution network operating at peak efficiency while preferably never surpassing in-house crude production capabilities.

Most Sinclair stations displaying a porcelain Sinclair "Dino" sign used a sign that was approximately 60" tall and 72" across at the widest point. Some smaller locations however, used a small version, shown here, that measured approximately 48" tall and 60" across. $300. *Jackie Knott Collection.*

Despite this potential problem, Sinclair was marching forward into the future. Futuristic modern porcelain station designs were introduced, and gasoline brand names underwent a realignment in the early 1960s. First off, Sinclair HC Gasoline, Sinclair's regular grade since 1934, was replaced in 1961 with Sinclair Dino Gasoline. Scarcely a year later, Sinclair Power-X was replaced by Sinclair Dino Supreme. Gas pumps graphics were redesigned, and, of interest to collectors, for the first time in their marketing history Sinclair specified a porcelain pump sign as part of their gas pump graphics package. Globes were redesigned, too, and the new Dino logo was added prominently to the design.

TBA marketing arrangements were strengthened, and Sinclair continued their long-standing ties to Goodyear. The selling of automotive parts and services was encouraged, and stations grew larger and larger to accommodate more types of automotive repair. In the early 1960s Sinclair continued the use of their long established motor oil brand names, Opaline and Pennsylvania, Extra Duty and Triple-X. In 1964 Sinclair's multi-grade, Triple-X, was replaced by an all new product, Sinclair Dino Supreme. Specialty lubricants and greases were offered for every conceivable automotive and industrial application. Agricultural products were also emphasized, and many new petrochemical applications were found for use by Sinclair's traditional rural customer base.

It wasn't all hard work and expansion, though. There was time for a little fun, even if it was at the expense of the company mascot. In 1964 Sinclair opened an exhibit at the New York World Fair, where life-sized dinosaurs, constructed of fiberglass, were brought together in a recreation of life as it was like in the Mesozoic Era. As the exhibit was being assembled, the dinosaurs toured much of Sinclair's marketing territory, and as the fair progressed, smaller versions of the dinosaurs were displayed at selected stations nationwide. The star of the show at the fair was Dino, a re-creation of Sinclair's brontosaurus mascot.

Sinclair TBA was supplied by Goodyear in the 1960s. Shown here is a dual-branded Sinclair Goodyear tin advertising sign. $250. *Jackie Knott Collection.*

1964 saw the end of an era when the Richfield jobber and dealer network was integrated into Sinclair's, and Sinclair signs replaced Richfield signs in fourteen East Coast states. Some jobbers were lost, however, in areas where the Sinclair was already represented. With this re-branding, the Sinclair trademark was again seen in New England.

Sinclair stations in the early 1960s that were authorized as truck stops displayed this sign as secondary identification. $350-$400. *Jackie Knott Collection.*

As the summer travel season geared up the following year, reality once again set in. Nationwide, petroleum marketing saw damaging price wars, competitive moves in which crude-rich companies, profiting from crude oil production and refining operations, chose to provide price supports to their dealer network, allowing them to sell gasoline below their published cost. Their effort was largely aimed at ridding the marketplace of independent gasoline "discounters," chain operated service stations that purchased refined gasoline on the open market and resold it at less than the major oil companies prevailing prices. While the price wars had the desired effect on many independents, major oil companies without sufficient crude production of their own as to allow crude profits to cover retail losses were caught in the crossfire. Many majors that had concentrated their marketing in the mid-continent area—Sinclair, DX, Pure, and others, would see profit losses from retail operations from which they would never recover.

As the sixties closed, the nation's interstate highway system continued to offer growth opportunities to aggressive gasoline marketers, and a co-operative travel bureau encouraged travelers to "See America Best By Car." Behind the scenes, though, those companies which were not self-sufficient in crude production, and those that had also been devastated by price wars, saw survival as their most pressing goal. Each company began to look around for possible merger partners, as did Sinclair.

This rest room cleanliness sign is laminated wood and dates from the 1960s. $150-$200. *Jackie Knott Collection.*

This incredibly detailed cast sign depicts the 1959 Sinclair "Dino" logo. $350. *Jackie Knott Collection.*

Scotchlite reflective material mounted over wood also depicts the 1959 Sinclair "Dino" logo. $250. *Jackie Knott Collection.*

Sinclair Dino Farm Center 1960s Farm Implements dealer sign. Tin, very rare. $600-$700. *Scott Benjamin Collection.*

Typical cardboard signage used to wrap around light poles in the 1960s. This one advertises Sinclair's new "Dino Supreme" motor oil, introduced in 1964, as well as a promotional game. $150. *Jackie Knott Collection.*

These signs identify Sinclair exploration leases and bear the logo that the exploration division used in the 1960s. $75-$125. Also shown is a pair of Sinclair Diesel pump plates used 1962-1970s. $75-$100. *Jackie Knott Collection.*

These porcelain signs were used on trucks and equipment belonging to Sinclair Oil and Gas, Sinclair's exploration division. The die-cut logo sign is available in both 4" ($600) and 10" (also $600). The 2" x 12" porcelain strip is valued at $200-$300. All items date from 1958 to 1970. *Jackie Knott Collection.*

Assorted Sinclair cans from the 1950s, 60s, and 70s. $20-$75. *Jackie Knott Collection.*

Sinclair 1966 oil can rack, filled with cans used in the 1966-1970 era. Rack and cans $150. *Jackie Knott Collection.*

When Sinclair H-C gasoline was renamed Sinclair Dino Gasoline in 1961, this hood was attached to gas pump globes to call attention to the new product. $200. *Jackie Knott Collection.*

These globes identified rest rooms in Sinclair station designs of the 1950s and 1960s. $35-$50. *Jackie Knott Collection.*

Two different Sinclair Lyon advertising dolls. $600-$800 each. *Jackie Knott Collection.*

Dino, long the Sinclair mascot, is seen here reproduced in miniature for various ornamental purposes. $25-$100. *Jackie Knott Collection.*

These miniature dinosaurs were offered in conjunction with Sinclair's displays at the 1964-65 New York World's Fair. $25. *Jackie Knott Collection.*

Sinclair promotional items, including so-called sign-pole thermometers that are very popular among collectors. $25-$50. *Jackie Knott Collection.*

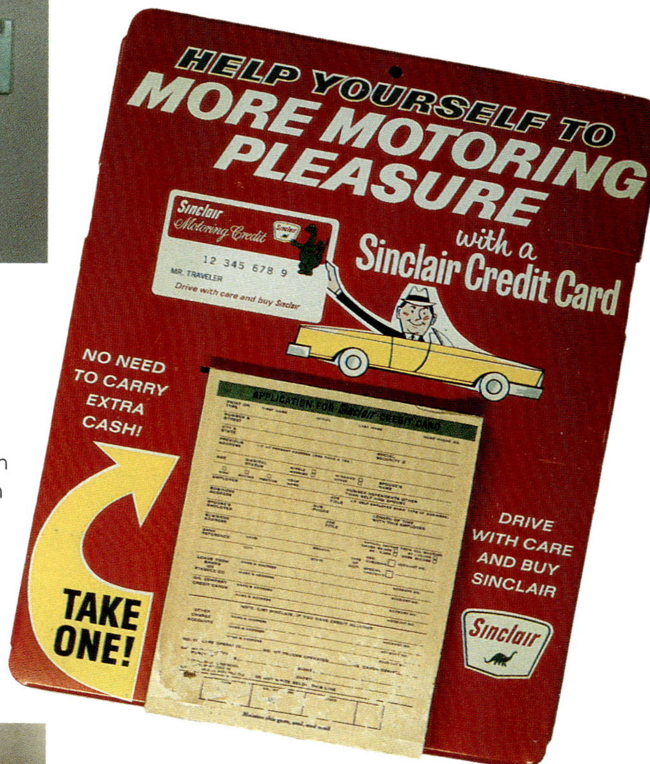

Use of proprietary credit cards increased tremendously in the 1960s. Motorists were encouraged to tear off an application and send it in for a Sinclair card. $50. *Jackie Knott Collection.*

Offered as a Christmas promotion for 1966, this Sinclair radio reproduces a Sinclair Dino Supreme Bennett 2000 series gas pump. $50. *Jackie Knott Collection.*

Generic ad glasses shown here along with a Sinclair Dino Gasoline glass, curved to fit a Bennett 966-1066 series pump. $25-$35. *Jackie Knott Collection.*

In the 1960s every oil company expanded their product line to include many additional specialty products for home and car. This display dates from the early 1960s. $25-$50. *Jackie Knott Collection.*

Extremely rare Dino and Dino Supreme ad glasses for Bennett 766 pumps (most were decals on older glass), along with curved (Bennett 966/1066) glass displaying the experimental "Hi Test HC" logo and the more familiar Dino Supreme. $25-$35. *Jackie Knott Collection.*

Sinclair's touring fiberglass dinosaurs are shown here at the grand opening of a Sinclair Travel Plaza in the 1960s. *Jackie Knott Collection.*

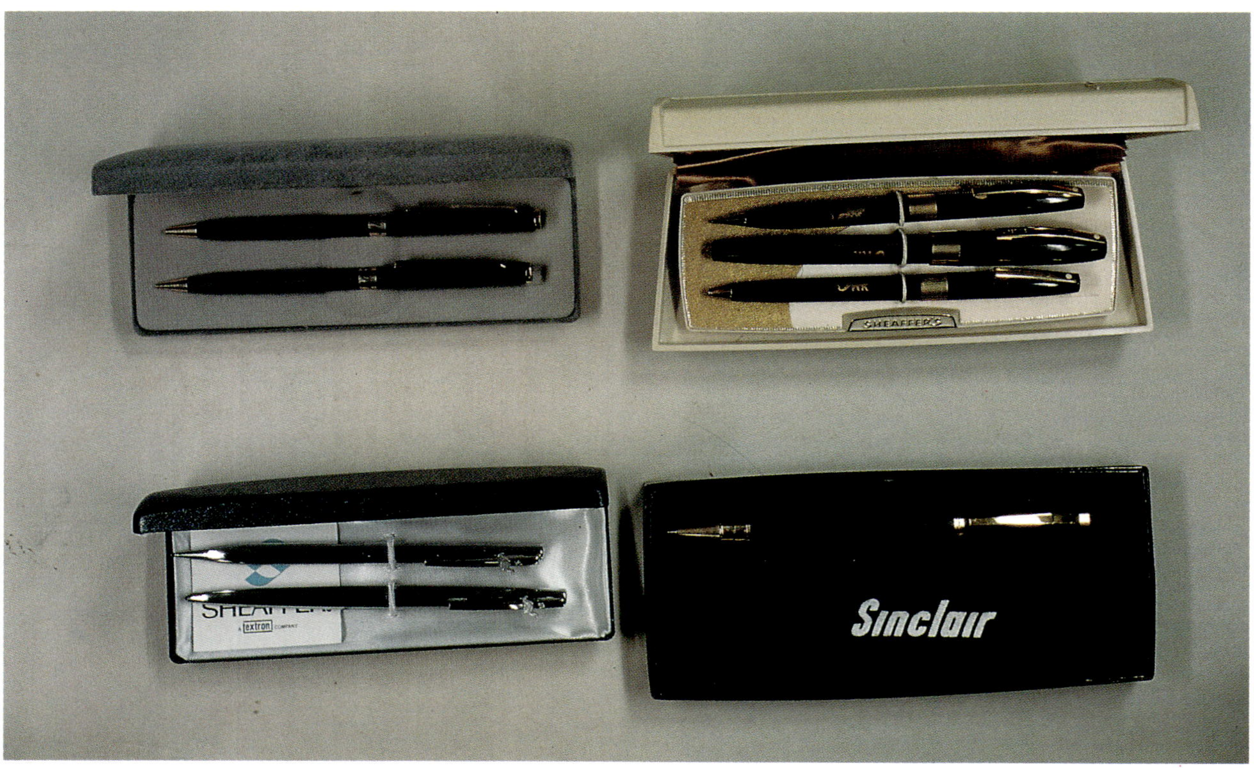

Presentation style Sinclair pens. \$25-\$100. *Jackie Knott Collection.*

Sinclair credit card receipt clipboards from the 1950s and 60s. $35. *Jackie Knott Collection.*

Specially marked oil cans, imprinted with prize notifications on the inside bottom, were designed so that service station driveway salesmen could participate in incentive promotions tied to motor oil sales. Shown here are specially imprinted bottoms removed from quart cans. $10. *Jackie Knott Collection.*

This porcelain credit card acceptance sign dates from the 1960s and was actually used, not at stations, but at motels and hotels that accepted the Sinclair credit card. $100. *Jackie Knott Collection.*

This porcelain credit card acceptance sign dates from the 1960s. $100. *Jackie Knott Collection.*

In the late 1960s the petroleum industry initiated the "Discover America Best By Car" campaign, intended to promote tourism and boost sales. Sinclair was an active participant, and this display includes various tourism products. $10-$50. *Jackie Knott Collection.*

Sinclair offered custom routing services to customers. This rack dispensed cards that motorists filled out and sent in for custom imprinted maps. $25. *Jackie Knott Collection.*

Company executives could even display corporate trademarks on their neckties. $25. *Jackie Knott Collection.*

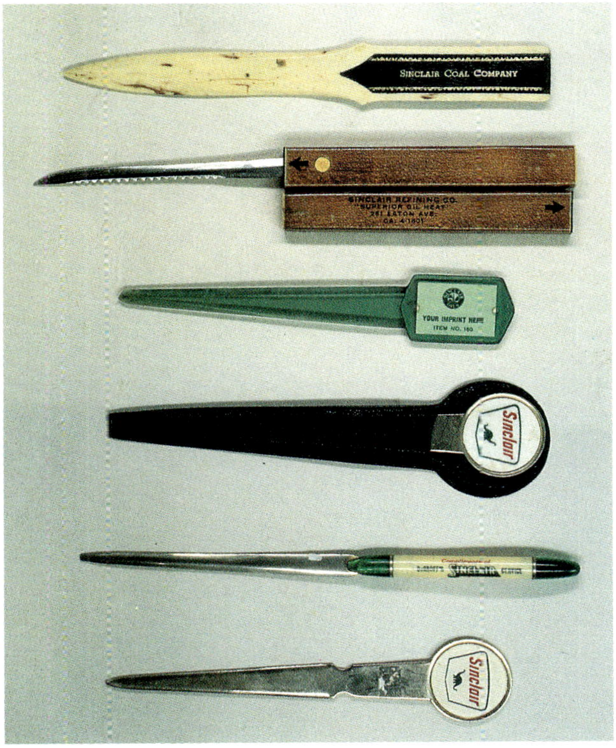

Letter openers display Sinclair trademarks through the years. $25-$100. *Jackie Knott Collection.*

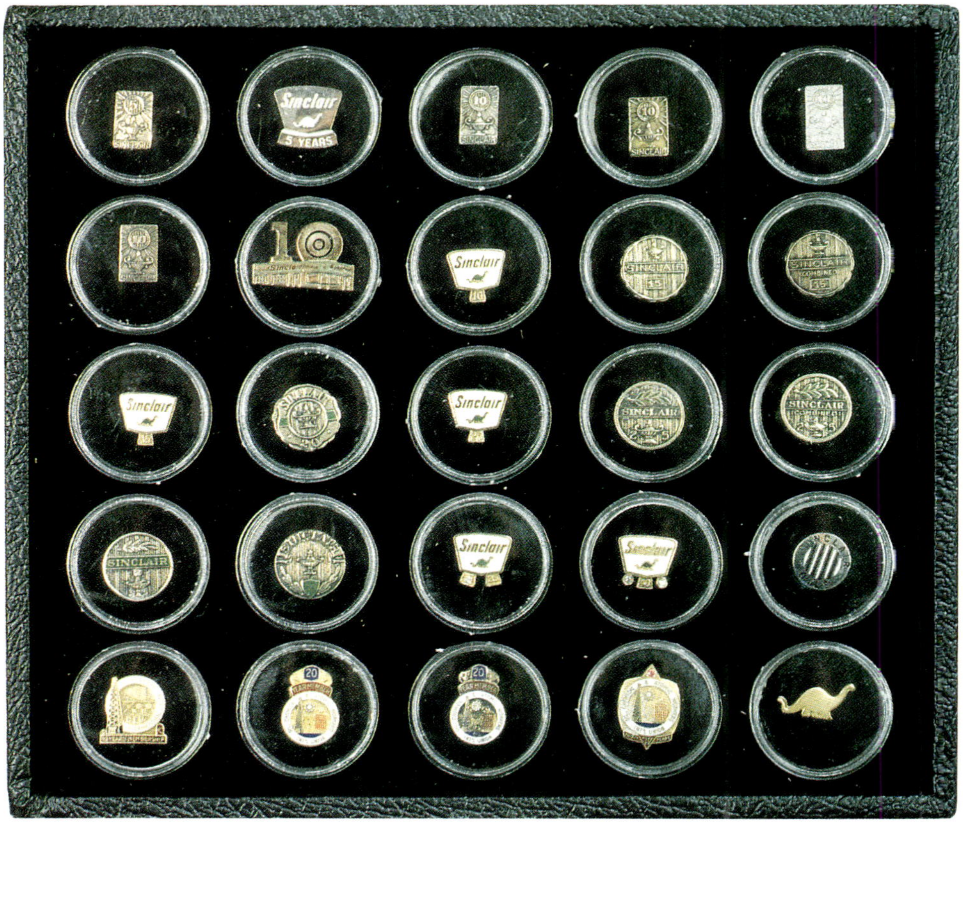

This display includes numerous Sinclair service award pins, a highly sought-after collectible. $100-$300. *Jackie Knott Collection.*

Assorted Sinclair promotional items. $25-$100. *Jackie Knott Collection.*

Shown here are playing cards adorned with various Sinclair logos. $10-$25. *Jackie Knott Collection.*

Coffee mugs and drinking glasses display the Sinclair logo. $10-$25. *Jackie Knott Collection.*

Among other Sinclair home use products of the 1960s was Sinclair Charcolite lighter fluid. $35. *Jackie Knott Collection.*

This wooden plaque displays the Sinclair "Dino" logo introduced in 1958. $100. *Jackie Knott Collection.*

This toy service station, originally generic, has been elaborately imaged as a Sinclair station of the 1960s. No listing. *Jackie Knott Collection.*

This tin-litho Sinclair "Dino" sign was used on Sinclair approach billboards. $100. *Jackie Knott Collection.*

This advertising poster dates from 1964-65 and advertises Sinclair's participation in the New York Worlds Fair. $35. *Jackie Knott Collection.*

This advertising poster promotes Sinclair's regular grade "Dino" gasoline in the early 1960s. $25. *Jackie Knott Collection.*

This advertising poster promotes Sinclair's regular grade "Dino" gasoline in the early 1960s. $25. *Jackie Knott Collection.*

This advertising poster promotes Sinclair's premium grade "Dino Supreme" gasoline in the early 1960s. $25. *Jackie Knott Collection.*

Sinclair's fuel oil program was branded "Super-Flame." This plastic Super-Flame sign dates from the 1960s. $35. *Jackie Knott Collection.*

In 1959 the newer italicized Sinclair logotype was added to the Sinclair HC globe design. $250. *Scott Benjamin Collection*

In 1961 Sinclair's regular grade gasoline, formerly HC, was renamed Sinclair Dino Gasoline, ending thirty-five years of the famed HC brandname. $175. *Scott Benjamin Collection.*

In 1962 Sinclair Power X was renamed Sinclair Dino Supreme. This globe advertises the new product. $200. *Scott Benjamin Collection.*

The italic Sinclair logotype was added to Sinclair Marine globes in the late 1950s. $450. *Scott Benjamin Collection.*

First offered in the mid-1960s, these inflatable Dinos have proved popular with children for over thirty years. About $15, at your neighborhood Sinclair station! *Scott Benjamin Collection.*

During the 1960s Sinclair sponsored a number of dinosaur-related functions and activities. Shown here are toy dinosaurs offered in conjunction with Sinclair's sponsorship of the New York World's Fair. $25. *Scott Benjamin Collection.*

Fiberglass replicas of dinosaurs were part of a Sinclair sponsored display at the 1964-65 New York World's Fair. This guide book identified the display replicas for visitors. $25.
Scott Benjamin Collection.

Every child in the 1960s played with Sinclair styled soap. $15-$25.
Scott Benjamin Collection.

The mid-1960s saw the development of this Sinclair porcelain station design. Sharp angular lines differ greatly from the earlier Sinclair prototypes, and a wall mounted identification sign was commonly used by many oil companies in the 1960s.

The Sinclair "Dino" sign was introduced in 1958, after several years of experimentation with various images to replace the dated "HC" logo.

The italic Sinclair logotype was added to Sinclair Diesel globes in the late 1950s. $225. *Scott Benjamin Collection.*

In the 1950s Sinclair experimented with various images to replace the dated "HC" logo. The invention of internally illuminated plastic signage clearly pointed out to petroleum marketers those images that were not clearly visible at a distance or did not light up well. This logo was introduced in 1958 and was in place at virtually every Sinclair station by the early 1960s. Show here is a typical 1960s internally illuminated Sinclair sign, found at Sikeston, Missouri, in 1990.

Atlantic Richfield and Sinclair

The beginning of the 1960s saw Atlantic Refining in much the same shape that Sinclair was in—a significant marketing investment without sufficient crude to supply the demand. To correct the deficiency, Atlantic chose to look for potential merger partners, oil companies that perhaps did not have the marketing presence that Atlantic had, but instead were more crude sufficient. Among the companies considered were Ashland Oil, with extensive domestic crude oil production, and Pure Oil, again with largely domestic reserves. Both mergers were abandoned, however, when it became apparent that anti-trust requirements would dictate that much of the overlapping marketing would have to be sold off. In 1965, however, Atlantic found a potential partner that was both crude sufficient and did not have overlapping marketing that would hinder the merger. That partner was none other than Richfield Oil Corporation. Not to be confused with Richfield Oil Company of New York, the Sinclair subsidiary that had been purchased by Sinclair in 1935 and absorbed into Sinclair in 1964. Richfield, independent since 1937, had sufficient crude production for both their own and as a supplement to Atlantic's refinery needs. And with stations in five West Coast states, the nearest Richfield station was over 1,000 miles from an Atlantic station. There would be no government interference, and in January 1966 the merger became a reality. Atlantic Richfield Company was born. While still operating under the Atlantic and Richfield brand names, a corporate identity, Arco, was being developed. In its infancy yet, Arco had the find of a lifetime in 1968 with the development of Alaska North Slope oil fields, from a base of operations at Prudhoe Bay. Arco, awash with crude, had reached the big time.

This clock promotes Sinclair motor oils in the 1970s. $35. *Jackie Knott Collection.*

Sinclair, still crude poor, was realizing a significant return on their Depression-era investment in Richfield when the Alaska oil was discovered. Seeing a light at the end of their crude-poor tunnel, Sinclair opted to merge with Arco in 1970. Unlike the Atlantic and Richfield merger from four years earlier, however, was the fact that the Justice Department would require divestiture of overlapping marketing assets. An arrangement was made with British Petroleum (who had also been involved with Alaska exploration and production) and in preparation for the merger, Sinclair stations in sixteen eastern states, primarily those areas where Atlantic also had stations, were re-branded BP.

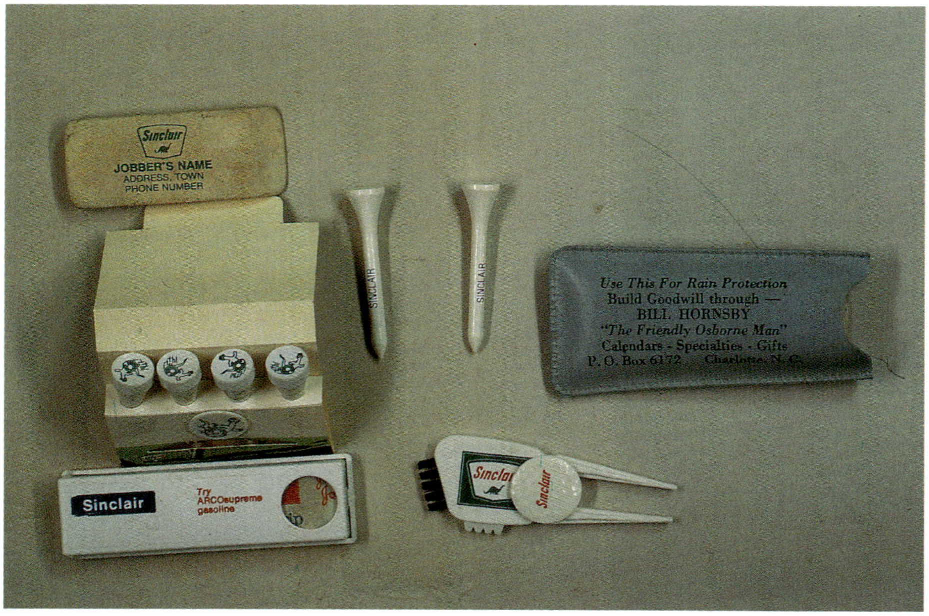

Various Sinclair promotional items, including a band-aid case from the Arco-Sinclair era. $25-$50. *Jackie Knott Collection.*

BP established a base of operations in Wilmington, Delaware, and the first BP signs went up at stations in Atlanta in 1969. The balance of the stations were scheduled for conversion to Atlantic Richfield's new "Arco" brand, then being introduced to replace Atlantic and Richfield. Despite the sell-off of eastern marketing, the Justice Department still was not satisfied with the Arco-Sinclair merger. At first, Arco agreed to maintain the Sinclair brand in the mid-continent area, and a unique blue rectangular Sinclair sign with the Arco spark was developed for use in these areas. By 1973, however, it was decided that Arco had to divest itself of all Sinclair retail marketing. But how? Remember that the mid continent marketing, the only portion of Sinclair that remained intact, had been through devastating price wars in the 1960s. What company could step in, absorb the remnants of Sinclair, and still see Justice Department approval? The answer would eventually see the rebirth of a strong Sinclair.

Drive With Care and Buy Sinclair...Sinclair high-rise sign along Interstate 44 at Rolla, Missouri.

In the late 1960s Sinclair developed a ranch style station for use at its ever-growing number of interstate interchange locations. This station stands along I-44 at Rolla, Missouri.

Manitou Springs, Colorado, is home to this modem, ranch-style Sinclair station. Set in a wooded area, even the dinosaur looks like he is at home here.

Author Wayne Henderson shown with his sister Nancy, ages seven and four, by a Sinclair sign in Gloucester Court House, Virginia, 1969. BP signage would replace this Sinclair sign later that year.

In some areas, the Arco brandname and product names replaced Sinclair. Shown here are pump toppers explaining the conversion to motorists. $25 each. *Wayne Henderson Collection.*

Rebuiling an Independent Giant

1973 marked the beginning of the greatest changes in petroleum marketing seen in this century. With the 1973-74 Arab embargo of crude, virtually every oil company found themselves in the same position that the "crude-poor" companies had just a few years before. Every marketer began concentrating their stations only in those areas where they could properly supply them, area in which they could be most profitable. Thousands of stations closed nationwide. Arco, under court order to divest itself of Sinclair, also chose to abandon the southeastern United States, as Arco stations in formerly strong Atlantic states such as Florida, the Carolinas, Georgia, and parts of Virginia were closed or sold. British Petroleum, still trying to make the former Sinclair marketing they had purchased profitable, sold stations in Florida, Georgia, and the Carolinas to American Petrofina, and Fina shields replaced BP signs at the former Sinclair outlets in these areas.

But what became of Sinclair? In those areas where Arco was forced to abandon the Sinclair operations, a large independent, Pasco, Inc., purchased control of Sinclair distribution and marketing assets and trademarks. They continued to operate stations under the Sinclair brand during the 1970s, and in 1976, Little America Refining Company, a Wyoming based refiner-marketer purchased the Sinclair brand, distribution facilities, and marketing properties in all states from the Mississippi River to the Rocky Mountains. Little America had long operated several tourist resorts in the Rockies and marketed gasoline under the Covey and Mobile brand names in Utah, Wyoming, and Idaho. Sinclair had supplied much of their refined products, and indeed the large stations at their resort properties were branded Sinclair.

Under the guiding hand of executives of Little America, Sinclair gradually began rebuilding. When Texaco withdrew from hundreds of stations in the upper Midwest in the late 1970s, Sinclair purchased and re-branded these properties. They entered the convenience store market, developing several successful store prototypes and strongly encouraging their jobber network to do likewise. Strong jobbers were solicited, and from this effort some of the largest jobbers in their territory converted from other brands to Sinclair.

The corporation was restructured again in 1986, when all of the Sinclair properties were fully merged into Little America and the Sinclair Oil Corporation was reborn. Today over 2,500 stations display the Sinclair "Dino" emblem that was first adopted in 1959. It is one of the oldest logos in use today in the petroleum industry. Sinclair stations are found in every state west of the Mississippi except for California and Oregon, as well as east of the Mississippi in Wisconsin, and some border area marketing in Illinois and Tennessee as well. Competitors look upon Sinclair as a first class operation, and their stations are often market leaders in towns where they are located.

Collector interest in the 1990s encouraged the creation of various toy trucks aimed at the collector market. Many of these accurately reproduce Sinclair graphics of their respective eras. $25-$100. *Jackie Knott Collection.*

Sinclair has discovered the magic of their trademark as well, and at many Sinclair outlets, Dino merchandise—toy trucks and airplanes, inflatable Dinos, and other display items are available. Nationwide, even in those areas where Sinclair hasn't marketed in over twenty-five years, the green brontosaurus, Dino, remains one of the most recognized trademarks ever, a trademark as timeless as the dinosaur itself.

Fantasy-reproduction Sinclair neon clock, created for today's collector market. No listing. *Jackie Knott Collection.*

Sinclair motor oils were promoted in this 1960s display. The cans shown are from a later era. $100 all. *Jackie Knott Collection.*

This clock displays Sinclair's logo and "Dino" image in the 1980s. $35. *Jackie Knott Collection.*

One of the primary factors in replacing the venerable Sinclair H-C logo was due to problems in proper illumination of plastic signage. In 1958 the Sinclair "Dino" logo was developed, and plastic signage was created using the new logo. Shown here is a plastic sign face from the 1970s. $100. *Jackie Knott Collection.*

Sinclair joined the other major oil companies in the 1990s in offering steel replica toy trucks. This promotional was available at Sinclair stations in 1989 and 1990. $50-$60. *Scott Benjamin Collection.*

Covey's "Little America" resort, Little America, Wyoming, about 1962. Sinclair gasoline was dispensed from fifty-five pumps at this location, a tourist resort hotel and restaurant facility. Little America Refining, an outgrowth of this operation, would eventually merge with the remnants of Sinclair left from the Arco merger, creating today's Sinclair Oil Corporation.

Author Scott Benjamin, shown here with a fiberglass display dinosaur in front of an Iowa City, Iowa, Sinclair station in August 1996.

Appendix One:

Sinclair & Richfield Pump Color Schemes

(Provided for the benefit of pump restoration efforts)

Sinclair

Sinclair specified no particular gas pump to fit any image era, although Sinclair did have a corporate arrangement with Bennett from the mid-1930s to 1970, and most Sinclair company owned stations used Bennett pumps. Jobbers were offered Bennett equipment at a discount, but were free to choose whatever equipment they wanted. The following color schemes apply to all makes of pumps carrying the brands indicated.

REGULAR 1920-1930: Sinclair Gasoline
Solid green pump, with Sinclair striped logo decal centered on door between dial glass window and base. Usually used an ad glass.

REGULAR 1930-1934: Sinclair Gasoline
Solid silver pump, with Sinclair striped logo decal centered on door between dial glass window and base. Usually used an ad glass.

PREMIUM 1926-1934: Sinclair HC
Solid red pump, with Sinclair HC decal centered on door between dial glass window and base. Usually used an ad glass.

MOTOR 1930-1934: Sinclair Pennant
Solid red pump, with Sinclair Pennant decal centered on door between dial glass window and base. Usually used an ad glass.

MOTOR 1930-1938: Sinclair US Motor Specifications
Solid white pump, with Sinclair striped logo decal centered on door between dial glass window and base. Usually used an ad glass.

REGULAR 1934-1946: Sinclair HC
Solid red pump, with Sinclair Ethyl decal centered on door between dial glass window and base. Usually used an ad glass.

PREMIUM 1934-1946: Sinclair Ethyl
Solid silver pump, with Sinclair Ethyl decal centered on door between dial glass window and base. Usually used an ad glass.

REGULAR 1946-1953: Sinclair HC
Green pump sides with 6" white band vertical from base to midpoint on center of side. White top and doors. Usually used an ad glass. Large round Sinclair HC decal centered on door between dial glass window and base.

PREMIUM 1946-1953: Sinclair Ethy
Red pump sides with 6" white band vertical from base to midpoint on center of side. White top and doors. Usually used an ad glass. Large round Sinclair Ethyl decal centered on door between dial glass window and base.

REGULAR 1953-1962: Sinclair HC
Green pump sides with 6" white band vertical from base to midpoint on center of side. White top and doors. Usually used an ad glass. Large round Sinclair HC decal centered on door between dial glass window and base. Smaller "RD-119" decal above HC.

PREMIUM 1953-1962: Sinclair Power X
Red pump sides with 6" white band vertical from base to midpoint on center of side. White top and doors. Usually used an ad glass. Large round Sinclair Power X decal centered on door between dial glass window and base. Smaller "RD-119" decal above HC.

DIESEL 1953-1960: Sinclair Diesel
Green pump sides and top with white door. Square porcelain pump sign with Sinclair Dino logo attached to door centered between dial glass window and base. Usually used ad glass for grade identification.

REGULAR 1962-1970: Sinclair Dino
White pump sides and top with green door. Square porcelain pump sign with Sinclair dino logo attached to door centered between dial glass window and base. Usually used ad glass for grade identification.

PREMIUM 1962-1970: Sinclair Dino Supreme
White pump sides and top with orange-red door. Square porcelain pump sign with Sinclair dino logo attached to door centered between dial glass window and base. Usually used ad glass for grade identification.

DIESEL 1960-1970: Sinclair Diesel
Green pump sides and top with white door. Square porcelain pump sign with Sinclair dino logo attached to door centered between dial glass window and base. Usually used ad glass for grade identification.

Note that in conjunction with the 1964 World's Fair, Sinclair's station at the fair site was equipped with some very unusual rocket shaped pumps constructed specifically for this location by Bennett.

Richfield Oil Company of New York

As an affiliate of Sinclair, Richfield used Bennett pumps wherever possible. Being a 100% jobber oriented marketer, pump selection was left to the individual jobber.

REGULAR 1939-1956: Richfield Hi-Octane
Creamy yellow pump with blue top and base. Twelve inch round Richfield Hi Octane decal centered on lower door between dial glass window and base. Usually used an ad glass.

PREMIUM 1939-1956: Richfield Ethyl
Creamy yellow pump with blue top and base. Twelve inch round Richfield Ethyl decal centered on lower door between dial glass window and base. Usually used an ad glass.

MOTOR 1939-1956: Rocor
Creamy yellow pump with blue top and base. Twelve inch round Rocor decal centered on lower door between dial glass window and base. Usually used an ad glass.

REGULAR 1956-1964: Richfield Hi-Octane
Creamy yellow pump with blue base. Rectangular "NEW/RICHFIELD HI- OCTANE /REGULAR PRICE" decal centered on lower door between dial glass window and base. Usually used an ad glass.

PREMIUM 1956-1964: Richfield Premium
White pump with 5" red vertical stripe painted across center of top and vertically down center of each door. Rectangular "SUPER/PREMIUM/RICHFIELD/HYDROGEN/POWERED" decal centered on lower door between dial glass window and base. Usually used an ad glass.

DIESEL 1956-1964: Richfield Diesel
Blue pump. Twelve inch round Richfield Diesel decal centered on lower door between dial glass window and base. Usually used an ad glass.

Appendix Two:

Quick Reference Guide

Sources of information, and times of further interest to collectors of Sinclair items and all forms of petroleum memorabilia.

ORIGINAL GLOBES

Oil Company Collectibles
Scott Benjamin
411 Forest Street
LaGrange, OH 44050
(216) 355-6608

NEW GLOBES ONLY

Lee Pergl
10985 Woodstock Road
Roswell, GA 30075
(770) 587-1822

NEW PUMPS ONLY

Benkin & Company
Ben and Steve Staub
14 East Main Street
Tipp City, OH 45371
(513) 667-5975

NEW PUMP PARTS, DECALS, CYLINDERS, NOSTALGIA ITEMS

Memories Restored
Luke Sconyers
301 South Main Street
Ashburn, GA 31714
(912) 567-9656

Time Passages
Scott and Debbie Anderson
P. O. Box 65596
West Des Moines, IA 50265
(800) 383-8888

Vic's Place
Vic and Sara Raupe
124 North 2nd
Guthrie, OK 73044
(405) 282-5586

Park Drive Garage
Andy Anderson
5734 South 86th Circle
Omaha, NE 68127
(402) 592-1710

Webers Nostalgia Supermarket
6611 Anglin Dr.
Ft Worth, TX 76119
(817) 534-6611

NEW DIAL FACES and ECO AIR METER PARTS

Ron Scobie
7676 120th St., North
Hugo, MN 55038
(612) 426-1023

TRADE PUBLICATIONS

Petroleum Collectibles Monthly
411 Forest Street
LaGrange, OH 44050
(216) 355-6608
FAX (216) 355-4955
The only complete monthly publication serving exclusively the petroleum collectibles hobby. PCM publishes the largest number of classified ads and includes the largest amount of general hobby information each and every month.
Visa, MC, AMEX accepted.

Mobilia
P. O. Box 575
Middlebury, VT 05753
(802) 545-2510

BOOKS

PCM Bookshelf
411 Forest Street
LaGrange, OH 44050
(216) 355-6608
FAX (216) 355-4955
Visa, MC, AMEX accepted.

GAS PUMP RESTORATION

Memories Restored
Luke Sconyers
301 South Main Street
Ashburn, GA 31714
(912) 567-9656

Vic's Place
Vic and Sara Raupe
124 North 2nd
Guthrie, OK 73044
(405) 282-5586

Park Drive Garage
Andy Anderson
5734 South 86th Circle
Omaha, NE 68127
(402) 592-1710

Bob Hull
31680 Mills Road
Avon, OH 44011
(216) 327-6097

Leonard Mort
P. O. Box 287
Millbury, MA 01527
(508) 865-3507

Gas Pump Ronnie
(909) 593-6336

Index

Acewood Petroleum 80
Agricultural products 128
Alaska North Slope oil fields 149
American Petrofina, Inc. 153
Arco spark 153
Arco, brandname of Atlantic Richfield Company 149
Arco-Sinclair merger 150
Ashland Oil Company 149
Ashland, brandname of Ashland Oil Company 80
Atlanta, Georgia 150
Atlantic Refining Company 39, 128, 149
aviation gasoline 40
Barber, W.H., brandname of The Pure Oil Company, U.S.A. 80
Belgium 35
Bennett Pump Company 156
Benzol 14
Betholine trademark 80
Betholine-Richfield brandname 86
Betholine-Richfield stations 80
Betholine-Sinclair brandname 86
BP, brandname of British Petroleum 80, 149
British Petroleum 80, 149
brontosaurus 86
Canada 35
Caribbean operations 8
Central Oil and Gasoline 13
Cities Service Oil Company 39
Colonial Beacon Oil Company 13
Conoco, brandname of Continental Oil Company 80
Consolidated Oil Corporation 38
convenience store market 153
Covey, brandname of Little America Refining 153
crude oil shortages 127
Cuba 35
Cudahy Refining 7
Cudahy, J. M. 6
Cushing, Oklahoma. 6
Dayton, Ohio 14
Detroit, Michigan 13
Dino 86, 128
Dino image 86
Dino merchandise 153
dinosaur trademark 5
dinosaurs 5
distribution network 127
DS, brandname of Western Oil & Fuel Company; and Continental Oil Company 80
DX, brandname of Sunray DX Oil Company 128
East Chicago, Illinois 8
East Chicago, Illinois refinery 8
England 35
Ethyl additive 14
Ethyl gasoline 14
Ethyl Gasoline Corporation 14
ethylized gas 14, 15
Europe 35, 40
experimental image 124
experimenting with plastic signage 85
expropriations by Mexico 35
Extra Duty Motor Oil 128
Fina, brandname of American Petrofina 153
Fort Wayne, Indiana 124
General Motors Research Labs 14
Glenn Pool, Oklahoma oil fields 6
Golden Tip, brandname of Stoll Refining Company 86
Goodyear 128
Great Depression 37, 39, 80
Greenwich, Connecticut 124
Gulf's first-ever station in Pittsburgh 13
H-C 15
High Compression 15, 123
Holland 35
Houston Concentrate 15
Independence, Kansas 38
independent gasoline "discounters" 128
inflatable Dinos 153
internally illuminated plexiglass signage 85
Isom, W. H. 8
Kansas City 8
Kansas frontier 5
Kayo, brandname of F.P. Kendall and Company; and Continental Oil Company 80
Keith Oil Company 13
Little America 153
Little America Refining Company 153
Louisville, Kentucky 86
Macon, Georgia 124
Mammoth Oil Company 37
Marcus Hook, Pennsylvania refinery 8
Maryland 80
Mesozoic Era 128
Mexican presence 35, 38
Mexico 8
mid-continent area 6
Mileage, brandname of Western Oil & Fuel Company and Continental Oil Company 80
Mobile, brandname of Little America Refining 153
Morristown, Tennessee 124
New England 80
New York 80
New York World Fair 128
Northern Europe 35, 40
oil exploration 6
Opaline Motor Oil 7, 128
Paraland, brandname of Phillips Petroleum 80
Parco, brandname of Producers and Refiners Corporation 38
Parco, Wyoming 38
Pasco, Inc. 153
Pennant, brandname of Pierce Petroleum 38
Pennsylvania 80
Pennsylvania Motor Oil 128
petrochemical 128
petroleum memorabilia 124
Phillips 66, brandname of Phillips Petroleum 80
Pierce Oil Company, S.A. 38
Pierce Petroleum 35, 38
porcelain sign 85
Prairie Oil and Gas 38
Premium Richfield 80
price wars 128
Producers and Refiners Corporation 38
Productos Sinclair "Red Rooster" 35
Productos Sinclair, brandname of Pierce Petroleum 38
Prudhoe Bay, Alaska 149
Pure, brandname of The Pure Oil Company, U.S.A. 128
Refiners Oil Company 14
refinery complex at Whiting, Indiana 8
Richfield Ethyl 80
Richfield Hi-Octane 80
Richfield jobber and dealer network 128
Richfield Oil Company of California 39, 80
Richfield Oil Company of New York 39, 80
Richfield Oil Corporation 39, 80
Richfield Oil Corporation 149
Richfield Truck Stops 86
Richfield, brandname of Richfield Oil Company of New York 80, 85, 86, 128
Rio Grande Oil Company 39
Salt Lake City, Utah 124
See America Best By Car campaign 128
Shell, brandname of Shell Oil Company 85
Sherwood Brothers 80
Sinclair "Castle" 40
Sinclair "greasing palaces" 13
Sinclair "Special" Gasoline 14
Sinclair "Triple Check" logo 124
Sinclair Aircraft 14
Sinclair Aircraft 15
Sinclair Benzol Motor Fuel 14
Sinclair Consolidated 37
Sinclair Consolidated Oil Corporation 8
Sinclair Dino Gasoline 127
Sinclair Dino Supreme 127, 128
Sinclair Extra Duty Triple X. 86
Sinclair Extra Duty 86
Sinclair farm products 13
Sinclair Gasoline 8, 13
Sinclair Gasoline (regular) 15
Sinclair Gulf Corporation 8
Sinclair HC (premium) 15
Sinclair HC Gasoline 15
Sinclair HC Gasoline logo 123
Sinclair HC with Ethyl 15
Sinclair Hi-Test HC 123
Sinclair Oil and Refining Company 7
Sinclair Oil Corporation 80
Sinclair Oil Corporation 153
Sinclair P.D. Stock Spray 13
Sinclair Pipe Line Company 37
Sinclair Power-X Gasoline 85, 123
Sinclair Tenol 86
Sinclair Truck Stops 86
Sinclair's "Greasing Palaces" 40
Sinclair's brontosaurus mascot 128
Sinclair, Harry F. 5
Sinco 8
speculators 6
St. Louis, Missouri 38
Standard "Red Crown" 14
Standard Of Indiana Solite 14
Standard Oil Company of Indiana 8, 14, 37
Standard Oil of New Jersey 14
Standard Oil The First 125 Years 37
Stoll Refining 86
striped HC logo 123
Super Par, brandname of The Pure Oil Company, U.S.A. 80
Supertest "High Compression" 123
Supertest Petroleum 36
TBA (Tires, Batteries, Accessories) 40
Teapot Dome 37
tetraethyl lead 14
Texaco, brandname of The Texas Company 153
The Pure Oil Company, U.S.A. 149
toy trucks, toy airplanes 153
Tri-State, brandname of Ashland Oil Company 80
Triple-X Motor Oil 128
Triverton, Rhode Island 13
Tulsa, Oklahoma 6
Union Petroleum Company 8
US Surgeon General 15
Virginia 80
Walburn Oil Company 39, 80
Washington, D.C. 80
Waters-Pierce Oil Company 38
Wilmington, Delaware 150
World War II 39, 85
Wyoming 37, 39